Decision Making

Decision Making

Proven Methods for Better Decisions

Paul E. Moody

McGraw-Hill Book Company

New York · St. Louis · San Francisco · Auckland
Bogotá · Hamburg · Johannesburg · London · Madrid
Mexico · Montreal · New Delhi · Panama · Paris
São Paulo · Singapore · Sydney · Tokyo · Toronto

Library of Congress Cataloging in Publication Data
Moody, Paul E.
  Decision making.

  Includes index.
  1. Decision-making. I. Title.
HD30.23.M65 1983   658.4′03′028   82-17196
ISBN 0-07-042868-9

1234567890   DOC/DOC   8987654321

ISBN 0-07-042868-9

The editors for this book were William R. Newton and Diane M. Krumrey,
the designer was Off-Broadway Graphics, and the production
supervisor was Sally Fliess. It was set in Aster
by University Graphics, Inc.
Printed and bound by R. R. Donnelley & Sons Company.

To my wife and best friend
Marilyn
and our three children
Kristann, Paul Jr., and Kathleen

ABOUT THE AUTHOR

Paul Moody received a B.S. degree in engineering from Lowell Technological Institute, Lowell, Massachusetts in 1958. His first position was that of a mechanical engineer working in the Design Division of the Portsmouth Naval Shipyard, Portsmouth, New Hampshire. He received a series of promotions in his technical field, culminating in a promotion in 1967 to a supervisory position. In 1970, Mr. Moody was promoted to a position at the Naval Underwater Systems Center (NUSC) in Newport, Rhode Island. He received an M.B.A. from the University of Rhode Island in 1977. Simultaneously, he attended a program which led to his being awarded an M.P.A. degree from the University of Northern Colorado in 1977. In addition to his full-time position at NUSC as a division head, he also teaches management courses at University of Rhode Island night school. Over the years, he has been the recipient of many awards.

Mr. Moody and his family reside in Barrington, Rhode Island.

Contents

Preface

Decisions are continually made by everyone. They range from the elementary decision a child makes when he or she decides to take a hand off a hot stove, to the complex decisions made when negotiating a SALT agreement. The range of decisions is truly vast and complex.

The purpose of this book is to present a guide as to how decisions should be made and the factors which influence decisions and decision makers. The book presents both an analysis of decision makers, some of the things that make them the way they are, and some of the processes which have been developed in order to assist the decision maker to quantify potential solutions.

In this book, the background of elemental decision making is presented first; the literature then proceeds with discussions of the decision makers and the impact of the human relations field on decision making, concluding with various decision-making techniques. Decision techniques start with the simple selection from two alternatives and proceed to the multialternative decision process where each alternative has a number of factors influencing the final selection. As a decision becomes more complex, so does the process involved in making a selection; however, there has been a conscious effort to keep the mathematics to a minimum. This book was prepared for the manager, not for the mathematician. The goal of the author is to make this book a reference source for management decisions rather than a quantitative analysis textbook.

Paul E. Moody

WE ARE ALL CONTINUALLY FACED

WITH A SERIES OF GREAT

OPPORTUNITIES, BRILLIANTLY DISGUISED

AS INSOLUBLE PROBLEMS

John Gardner

Decision Making

Chapter **1**

Introduction

DECISION LOOP

Often it has been asked whether organizations have any rules and regulations that relate to a process by which a manager can arrive at objectives, policies, and strategies. While there is no single set of rules for any of these functions, they all relate to decisions of different forms. Although a number of authors have tried to compile a concise list of rules to fit all cases, their attempts have been futile. However, a series of steps can be listed that relate to all decision-making circumstances. Figure 1 illustrates the closed-loop decision process.

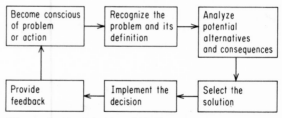

Figure 1   Decision-making loop.

The decision may be simplistic or complex, or it may relate to any of the other fields of management; however, all decisions can be guided by the basic closed-loop process.

IMPORTANCE OF THE DECISION

How are most decisions made? Are they made by guessing, by taking a poll, by voting, by following a hunch, by experience, or by a systematic approach to determine the best way to solve a particular problem? If this were a multiple-choice quiz, we would have to check the block that indicates all the above.

Given that a number of methods can be used to arrive at a decision, how can we determine which one to use at a particular time? Obviously, this problem relates to the importance of the decision. For example, in an average business day, a decision as to which letter to answer first may be inconsequential, and so it may be made on a first-in, first-out basis. However, a decision related either to the selection of an individual for a major management position or to a significant capital expenditure would require significant prior research. Are there any guidelines to help determine the importance of a decision? Research indicates that there are guidelines for almost everything. Do we need them? The answer depends on the particular situation. In this text we provide these guidelines in a "cookbook" fashion for those times when they are needed. Thus the time required to read long-winded presentations of information (with the facts cleverly concealed) can be saved; instead, you can refer to lists that can be referenced with a minimum of digging.

The decision maker not only must make correct decisions, but also must make them in a timely manner at minimum cost. The minor decisions may not warrant thorough analysis and research and even may be safely delegated to others. The importance of a decision is strongly related to the decision maker's position in the organization. For example, a decision that may be of minor importance to a top executive may be of major importance to the individual making the choice at a lower level.

To assess a decision's importance, five factors should be evaluated:

1. *Size or Length of Commitment.* If the decision entails the commitment of considerable capital or the expenditure of great effort by a number of people, then it is considered a major decision. Similarly, if the decision will have a long-term impact on the organization, such as relocating a plant to a new or foreign site or getting into or out of a particular segment of the market, the decision is considered major.

2. *Flexibility of Plans.* Some plans can be reversed easily, while others have a degree of finality about them. If a decision involves taking a course of action that cannot be reversed easily, then that decision assumes major significance. An example would be the selling of patent rights for an invention that a company is not using presently but may wish to use in the future; another example would be the sale of a piece of land that is not being used currently. The financial consideration may be minor at the time of sale, but the long-term impact on the company may be significant.

3. *Certainty of Goals and Premises.* If a company has a long-standing policy of acting in a certain situation in a particular way, then it is easy to make a decision that is consistent with past history. However, if an organization is very volatile and a historical pattern has not been established—or if the nature of the decision is such that actions are highly dependent on factors known to only higher-level personnel in the organization—then the decision assumes major importance. For example, it would be quite inappropriate for financial directors to declare the amount of dividends to be paid based solely on their own financial data. They may not be aware of a capital expenditure that the company's top management has been considering while waiting for adequate profit data to justify the investment.

4. *Quantifiability of Variables.* When the costs associated with a decision can be defined accurately, the decision takes on minor importance. For example, if the method by which a component is to be machined must be chosen and if the cost and time associated with the use of each method are known, then the analysis of relevant factors and the resulting decision are not very important. But if the decision is related to bidding on the design and manufacture of a complex item and if the cost and program relate to a broad estimate which is subject to errors, then the decision assumes much greater importance.

5. *Human Impact.* Where the human impact of a decision is great, its importance is great. This is particularly true when the decision involves many people. As an example, I once worked in an organization that had two major facilities approximately 100 miles apart. To consolidate operations, it was decided to move one particular function from one location to the other. This may have been a fine plan; however, it did not take into account the fact that approximately 250 employees would have to either move or commute 100 miles. When top management finally realized the impact of the plan in terms of unhappy people and the potential of many of the best people for finding other employment, the plan was scrapped.

TIME-COST RELATIONSHIP

How do we make these final decisions? How much data do we gather first? How much does the data cost? Why can some people not make decisions even after great anguish over the alternatives? These questions relate to the individual's background, or experience, and education.

Although there is little we can do to change our personalities or out-looks on life, and we only have hindsight in relation to our personal experiences, we can do a lot about future life and educational experiences. This text could be one step of an educational experience that will continue for the rest of our lives, for one primary difference between a "success" and an "almost success" relates to an individual's ability to make timely and good decisions, regardless of the complexity of the problem or the decision maker's experience with it.

Let's start by developing a definition of a decision. For the purposes of this text, a *decision* is an action that must be taken when there is no more time for gathering facts. The problem is how to decide when to stop gathering facts. The solution varies with each problem we attempt to solve, for gathering facts costs time and money.

Figure 2 graphically elucidates the cost of gathering facts versus the benefits derived. In Figure 2, the more time expended gathering facts,

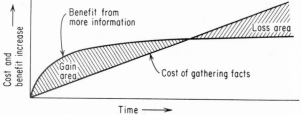

Figure 2   Cost-benefit time curves.

the greater the total related cost. Note that this loss may be felt in terms of not only money but also opportunity, effectiveness of action, reversibility of a decision, and so on. Also there is an immediate benefit from having additional data to help us make the decision. However, as time goes on, the marginal benefit decreases until finally we have waited too long. The cost associated with gathering facts has outweighed the benefit that they provide. In essence, we move from a position where we could gain by the accumulation of data to one in which we lose.

This type of chart varies radically for each decision; however, the principle remains unchanged. For example, the time required for a child to take her hand off a hot stove may be quite dramatic relative to the cost in terms of pain and the benefit in terms of the burn's severity. Conversely, a decision to sign or not sign a SALT agreement does not have a similar short time frame, and much data gathering is required. But, even with a SALT agreement, too much delay may result in additional problems which could be more serious than we care to think about now.

If excessive gathering of facts is a risk, then why do it? The answer is evident. We gather facts to limit uncertainties about the results of the course of action we choose. For every decision made, there are varying amounts of uncertainty. Our task is to reduce that uncertainty until we are reasonably certain of the results of different options without exceeding the crossover point of cost versus benefit. An example of the relationship between uncertainty and the cost of gathering data is illustrated in Figure 3.

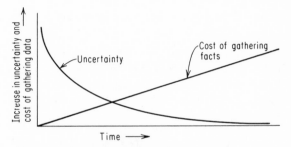

Figure 3 Cost-uncertainty time curves.

As previously illustrated, the cost of gathering data increases with time. However, as time passes and the amount of data gathered increases, uncertainty decreases. Note that uncertainty never reaches zero. So do we keep gathering facts until the uncertainty curve has flattened out? Not at all. By that time it is quite possible that we have passed our crossover point between cost and benefit and time has passed us by.

Now we are back to the beginning. How do we make effective decisions given that uncertainty will always be with us and that reducing this uncertainty entails a cost? The answer is to first analyze the problem and then evaluate its relative magnitude. For minor problems, off-the-cuff decisions may be completely proper. For decisions having major ramifications, the proper amount of data must be gathered to select the best course of action. Another way to look at the time versus uncertainty curve is to compare it with the curve of total cost of obtaining data to reduce uncertainty versus actual cost savings derived from the additional data. See Figure 4.

The point is that normally the total cost can be reduced by the improved decisions made after data have been gathered. However, at a certain point the cost of gathering data does not marginally improve

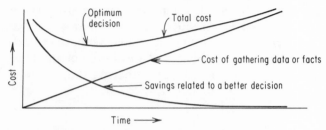

Figure 4   Optimum decision point curves.

the cost factor associated with an improved decision. On Figure 4 this point is called the *optimum decision* point. Delaying the decision any longer results in a total increased cost, which may be in terms of actual dollars, opportunity costs, or other factors.

ELEMENTS OF THE DECISION PROCESS

In *The Effective Executive*[1] Peter Drucker lists five elements of the decision process:

1. Clear realization that the problem is generic and can be solved only through a decision that establishes a rule
2. Definition of the specifications of the solution, or the *boundary conditions*
3. Derivation of a solution that is "right," that is, one that fully satisfies the specifications before attention is given to the concessions needed to make the decision acceptable
4. The building into the decision of the action to carry it out
5. The *feedback* that tests the validity and effectiveness of the decision against the actual course of events

[1]Peter E. Drucker, *The Effective Executive*, New York, Harper & Row, Publishers, Incorporated, 1967.

Drucker goes on to explain that a decision is a judgment and, as such, is rarely a choice between right and wrong. At best, it is a choice between "almost right" and "almost wrong."

Clearly, decisions involve compromise; but I cannot agree that a particular set of steps can be followed to arrive at "almost right" conclusions. The reason is that almost all decisions are unique in character, controlling conditions, and preferred resolution. The best that any text can offer a manager or decision maker is, first, enough data to induce that person to consider the situation as a decision point, to recognize that a number of studies and investigations have been conducted which may provide guidance in arriving at the optimal decision, and, second, a single, readable (not high-powered) method of analyzing alternatives.

DECISION INGREDIENTS

The art—not science—of decision making is based on five basic ingredients.

1. *Facts*. In this text we discuss some methods of obtaining facts. Facts are gathered for both sides of the question, pro and con, in order to define the boundaries of the problem. However, if facts cannot be obtained, the decision must be based on the available data, which fall into the category of general information.

2. *Knowledge*. If the decision maker has knowledge of either the circumstances surrounding the problem or a similar situation, then this knowledge can be used in selecting a favorable course of action. In the absence of personal knowledge, we are forced to seek advice from those who are informed. Thus there has been a tremendous increase in the consulting business. In the 1920s and 1930s, a manager was expected to be familiar with all aspects of the business. However, this expectation has declined in recent years as business has grown more complex and individuals have specialized in areas in which a general manager could not be expected to possess technical knowledge, owing to the years of training needed. Obtaining consulting services is even more important when more than one speciality is involved in the analysis of multiple aspects of a complex problem.

3. *Experience*. When an individual solves a problem in a particular way and the results are either poor or good, that experience provides him or her with data to use in solving the next similar problem. If an acceptable solution is found, most likely it will be repeated each time a similar problem arises. If we lack experience, then we have to experiment, but only when the results of a bad experiment do not have disastrous consequences. Major problems, though, cannot be solved by experiment.

4. *Analysis.* A great deal of the following text is devoted to methods of analyzing problems. These methods should supplement, but not replace, the other ingredients. However, in the absence of a method to mathematically analyze a problem, perhaps we can study it by other than mathematical means; if that fails, we must rely on intuition. Some people scoff at intuition. But if the other ingredients of decision making do not point to a direction to take, then intuition may be the only choice left.

5. *Judgment.* Judgment is needed to combine the facts, knowledge, experience, and analysis to select the proper course of action. There is no substitute for good judgment.

DECISION CHARACTERISTICS

There are five characteristics of decisions. The first two are quite similar to the factors used to evaluate a decision's importance.

1. *Futurity.* This characteristic involves the extent to which commitment entailed by the decision will affect the future. A decision that has a long-term influence can be considered a high-level decision, whereas a short-term decision can be made at a much lower level.

2. *Reversibility.* This factor relates to the speed with which a decision can be reversed and the difficulty involved in making that reversal. If reversibility is difficult, a high-level decision is indicated; but if reversibility is easy, a low-level decision is needed.

3. *Impact.* This characteristic relates to the extent to which other areas or activities are affected. If the impact is extensive, then a high-level decision is indicated; a singular impact relates to a low-level decision.

4. *Quality.* This factor relates to labor relations, ethical values, legal considerations, basic principles of conduct, company image, and so on. If many of these factors are involved, a high-level decision is needed; if only a few factors are relevant, a low-level decision is indicated.

5. *Periodicity.* This element relates to whether the decision is made frequently or rarely. A rare decision is a high-level decision, whereas a frequently made decision is a low-level decision.

DECISION PROBLEMS

The next topic to discuss is the 10 greatest problem areas associated with decision making. It may not be the best form to start a text with a series of lists. However, the purpose here is not to present data that should be taken as gospel, but rather to emphasize that many aspects must be considered in decision making and no one view represents the entire picture.

1. *Misdirection.* This is a case of wrong question, right answer. As an example, suppose you were looking for a top scientist to lead a group of highly trained technical personnel in search of a major breakthrough in some scientific field. You may find and hire the top scientist, only to have him or her lead the program into complete chaos and disorganized research projects. Perhaps you did not need a top scientist at all; what you needed may have been an individual with a scientific background and a record of success in getting technical people to work together to accomplish a joint objective.

2. *Sampling.* This problem involves the difficulty of securing a sample that is both adequate and representative. This is a constant problem in marketing, for an entire field of expertise has been developed to obtain sample sizes from a portion of the population which reflect what can be expected from the entire population. Although statistical analysis offers all sorts of probability curves and analytical data, there is the ever-present danger that the sample taken may not represent the facts. The most famous example of the danger of sampling is the major automobile manufacturer that took samples to determine exactly what the U.S. public wanted in an automobile. The difficulty arose because what people claimed they wanted was quite different from what they actually wanted. The result was the Edsel.

3. *Bias.* This factor is the degree to which prejudice affects the answers. Although bias may be found in the decision maker, in a major decision the decision maker may well depend on information from a source having an unidentified bias. One example comes from my own experience when I applied for a position in a research laboratory at a particular salary. I was hired at the salary I requested; however, not until years later did I learn that one of my coworkers had recommended that I be offered a much lower starting salary. When I asked why, he stated that he thought I would turn it down, and he was not in favor of hiring any competition for himself. Fortunately for me, the man who made the final decision saw through this bias.

4. *Ubiquitous Average*. Averages bury extremes, and these extremes may be very important. For example, assume you are considering going into a business which has a 10 to 50 percent profit on various items with an average return of 20 percent. You discover that you can expect your accounts receivable to be paid anywhere from 30 days to a year, with an average account being paid in 60 days. From the straight mathematics of the business, based on averages, it may appear to be a good investment. However, once into it, you may find that your low-profit items are paid promptly whereas collecting on high-profit items takes considerable time. This could force you to borrow capital to stay in business. The cost of the borrowing could change what appeared to be a good deal, based on averages, to a bad deal, based on reality.

5. *Selectivity*. This factor involves rejecting unfavorable results or choosing a method that is certain to yield favorable answers. The most common example of selectivity is a politician commenting on the results of primary elections. A candidate can lose 10 out of 12 districts in a primary and appear quite sincere when noting that the two trend-setter districts are indications that a groundswell of support is developing. Another example of obtaining a selective answer is the circulation of a marketing sampler that asks questions such as, Would you prefer to feed your children the higher-priced, yet nourishing breakfast food brand X or the lower-priced brand Y which has no nutritional value?

6. *Interpretation*. There is the danger in using facts and arriving at a distortion of their meaning. The most common problem associated with interpretation is simply the lack of technical background to understand what the facts mean. For example, the difference between a statistical and an actual sample could be expressed via the *mean*, the *median*, or the *mode*. If you were not familiar with the terms, you might think they all meant the same thing. In reality, they imply different things, and you may be considerably more interested in one than in the other, depending on the problem being evaluated.

7. *Jumped-at Conclusion*. You build it, walk into it, and spring it all by yourself. No one sets the trap for you. This is a simple trap to fall into, especially if you already favor a particular solution and the first bit of data substantiates your "gut feeling." Take the college professor who was correcting final examinations and happened to correct the class clown's paper first. The paper received a grade of 40 percent, so the professor immediately marked the class clown's report card with an F. What does the professor do after discovering that the 40 percent is the top grade for the class? Or there is the much more famous example of the embarrassed New York newspaper that ran a headline, following a Presidential election, that Dewey defeated Truman.

8. *Meaningless Difference.* A lot can be done to avoid this problem by practical experience. Suppose a company decides to invest considerable capital resources in buying an expensive computer system in which the staff has a considerable degree of capability and excellent technical background. In a field that changes as rapidly as the computer field, the technological edge of today may be completely meaningless tomorrow. So the option of renting computer services should be seriously considered before any large capital investment is made.

9. *Connotation.* This problem relates to an emotional content or implication that is added to an explicit literal meaning. Connotations can easily mislead the decision maker who is not aware of and watching out for them on a continuous basis. This emotional connection is used every day in advertising media. Take, for example, the names of models of automobiles. They imply romance, intrigue, speed, adventure, and so on. The story comes to mind of the boy who offered his little brother one *great big nickel* in exchange for two little dimes.

10. *Status.* In a business environment there is a barrier between a supervisor and a subordinate which limits communication in either direction. There is the fear of disapproval, on the one hand, and the fear of loss of prestige, on the other. This barrier can be low or high; however, the decision maker must recognize that it is always there and will have considerable impact on the data transmitted. In literally hundreds of conversations with both supervisors and subordinates, I cannot remember one in which one of us said, "Well, here is the data; however, it may be completely wrong."

SUMMARY

In this chapter we introduced the concept of the decision loop. Then we discussed how the importance of a decision relates to the speed with which we proceed through this loop. We also discussed factors that differentiate between an important and a routine decision.

Next we reviewed the cost of gathering data and the increase in benefits derived from this additional information. As more and more data is collected, the risk of uncertainty decreases. However, at a certain point the cost of gathering data does not increase the effectiveness of the final decision, and any further delay would pass the optimum decision point and increase total costs.

We talked about decision process elements as outlined by a prominent expert in the field. We supplemented this with a list of decision ingredients and characteristics. Finally, we listed 10 problems associated with the decision process that should be recognized and avoided.

Chapter 2

Decision Makers

RISK AND COMMITMENT

One of the interesting theories related to decision makers is that an individual's preference to the assumption of risk is inversely proportional to the size of the commitment involved in a decision. This concept is illustrated graphically in Figure 5. In this figure the average individual is not very concerned about making a high-risk decision when the com-

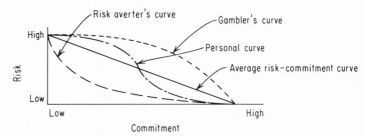

Figure 5   Risk-commitment curve.

mitment is relatively low. The curve also indicates that the average individual does not become involved in a high-commitment endeavor unless the risk is relatively low. An example is the purchase of a lottery ticket, which has a very high risk (in that most likely it will not win); yet the investment is low. But very few people would buy a home without first inspecting it, to make sure they were getting sufficient value for the high investment involved.

However, very few of us fit into what may be considered the average curve. Figure 5 indicates that some people may be willing to make a much greater commitment at higher risk than the average individual. This is indicated by the gambler's curve. Other people are much more timid than the average individual and make a significant commitment only when the risk has been reduced considerably. This type is represented by the risk averter's curve.

To assess an individual's preference within the total number of possibilities, we must understand the individual's background and position within the organization. For example, a higher-level manager may be accustomed to taking larger risks than a lower-level manager. Another factor is the possible impact of the decision on the company or on the personal fortune of the decision maker. One person may be more conservative with a company's funds while another may be more conservative with her or his own fortune. We cannot say that one is right and the other wrong, because the circumstances of each case are unique. Nonetheless, for a particular type of business, it would be wise to watch both the successful and unsuccessful managers and try to categorize their management styles with regard to risk versus commitment; then, of course, emulate the successful manager.

The last curve shown in Figure 5 is the personal curve, which represents the majority of us, in that we all tend to accept a high risk as long as the commitment is low. However, once the commitment increases to such a point that we feel threatened by that high a commitment, we wish to reduce the risk as much as possible. The trick of finding the best risk-commitment curve is to select one in which you are not such a risk averter that you miss opportunities, but you are not such a gambler that your actions become dangerously risky relative to your ratio of right to wrong decisions.

SCIENTIFIC DECISION MAKERS

If decisions are made at all levels of an organization, who can be called the decision makers? The answer is that everyone working in a business environment is a decision maker. Will this continue? Some say "Yes," others "No."

In the early days of the industrial revolution, the owner or manager of a business ruled with an iron fist. A decision made by the boss always was right. No questions—no problems. However, as the working class became more educated, they realized that the boss was just another person, whose decisions could be good or not so good, like anyone else's. As management realized that business was becoming more complex, they hired experts to advise them in the fields of law, government, finance, engineering, marketing, computers, manufacturing, unions, and so on. The list is endless for a very diverse company. Where does it end? In the early 1900s the decision maker's choices were based primarily on operating statistics and internal data. Since this method proved to lack the sophistication needed to cope with the array of factors related to a major decision, how could management possibly afford all the expertise needed (theoretically) to solve a problem?

Academicians offered an answer—*operations research*. Many claim that, with the techniques of operations research, empirically derived data can be applied to any problem to weigh alternatives, predict outcomes, and eventually replace the manager as a decision maker. Figure 6 illustrates this concept with respect to time.

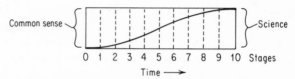

Figure 6   Science versus common sense decision trend.

The idea is that we progress from stage to stage over time. Although scientists were minimally useful in the early 1900s, their influence grows with time. This is an interesting yet false concept, for the amount of data and the number of variables that must be used in the analysis demand that the data be interpreted before they are employed in the solution of the problem. As the old saying goes, "Figures don't lie—but liars figure." Determining what data to feed into the operations analysis computation is still a commonsense procedure. Therefore, the analysis is more of a tool than a replacement for the decision maker.

If we accept the premise that operations research will not replace the decision maker, then it may help to scrutinize the decision maker and discuss some psychological theories related to his or her makeup.

ECONOMIC MAN

Theories of decision making frequently assume that the decision (at least the business decision) is based on marginal economics. And thus the decision maker, being an *economic man*, tries to maximize profits given his ability, the law, and personal ethical standards.

However, this economic man theory is being replaced by the viewpoint of many modern business analysts, who believe that modern decision makers do not try to maximize profit, but seek only an "adequate" profit that satisfies the other requirements in the overall decision. The decision maker may be quite reluctant to move toward a high-payoff venture if it is against company policy or might require the company to get into a new field, might cause an organizational change, and so on. Only some drastic event would cause this type of manager to choose a path drastically different from the norm. An example is the change in a company's policies following the loss of a chief executive who had been running the company into the ground.

The modern decision maker might say that what looks like "adequate profit" seeking may be, in reality, long-term profit maximization. This argument takes into account that short-term profit maximization can result in a violation of the law, can attract competition, or can lose the goodwill of the customers. In addition, some decision makers try to keep things on an even keel, rather than assume higher risks, because higher risks normally entail more work. Remember, a decision maker is an individual and so has the normal human weaknesses and strengths.

A decision maker may not be a profit maximizer because he or she associates the wrong item with profit. For example, increased sales do not always mean increased profit when the related expenses of over-time, transportation, and bonuses are taken into account. Diversification does not indicate increased profit when some of the new lines are losers. Reduced production costs do not imply increased profit when quality is sacrificed and sales drop. Highly paid professional managers do not necessarily bring greater profits when the economic man makes decisions from a personal viewpoint rather than that of the company, or when the managers' salaries are high enough to significantly impact the company's profit. This latter factor may be related to the fact that, in modern corporations, often ownership is quite separate from management, and the manager, hoping to move on to bigger and better things, may strive for a short-term indication of his or her contribution.

Usually increased sales mean increased profit, as do lower costs. Therefore, any company that traditionally raised its profits by increasing sales would be quite threatened by the thought of diminished sales. Tradition can operate in either direction, and a common exception to the rule is the company that specializes in high-quality goods for a small portion of the total market. One company that has thrived on this high-quality, high-price theory is Rolls-Royce. Rolls-Royce believes not only that there always will be a market for superbly engineered automobiles, but also that an inferior component, however cheap, could never be justified if a better (yet more costly) product could be created.

The individual decision maker must combine the company's tradition with personal needs. If there is a serious clash, usually the decision maker moves on. If not, the decision maker may combine her or his personal beliefs with the company's tradition and arrive at an almost predictable decision.

CATEGORIES OF DECISION MAKER

Some decision makers are so predictable in their approach to solving a problem that they can be categorized. These are some of the categories:[1]

1. The economic, who is interested in only what is useful and practical
2. The aesthetic, whose highest values lie in harmony and individuality, pomp and power
3. The theoretical, interested in the discovery of truth for its own sake and in diversity and rationality
4. The social, who loves people, considers other people as ends, and is kind, sympathetic, and unselfish
5. The political, who is interested primarily in power, influence, or renown
6. The religious, whose highest value is the greatest spiritual and absolutely satisfying experience, an ascetic who seeks experience through self-denial and dedication

It is hard to believe that anyone is a pure example of one of these types, for most people are mixtures. However, the dominant components have an important effect on a person's decision making. At this point, ask yourself whether you fall into one of these categories more than the others. If you do, then you must recognize that your decisions may be biased in a direction that will not always yield an optimum decision. For example, a type 1 decision maker might favor immediate profits in lieu of research, whereas a type 3 might be interested in research regardless of its potential end use. The type 2 person might do well in a company that stresses quality, as long as she or he did not stress quality to the point where the company was losing money. The type 4 decision maker is usually a very popular manager. This can work in two ways. First, a person's popularity can bring out the best in coworkers. Second, a type 4 may set standards that are very easy to meet. A type 5 person, while likely to be a very good decision maker, may make

[1]Edward Spanger and Max Niemeyer, *Types of Men*, Halle and Saale, Publishers, 1922.

choices that favor his or her portion of the company rather than the entire company. A type 6 decision maker is unlikely to get involved with business decisions. As stated previously, decisions must be made in relation to a large variety of variables; a good decision maker should have a balanced outlook so that his or her approach will be impartial.

One means of evaluating your own decision-making capability is to place yourself in each of the six categories (one at a time) and then decide what action you would take on a particular problem. If you do this exercise properly, you might consider alternatives that you would not have imagined had you not tried to categorize your action. Possibly one of these decision-making methods may give you insight into which type is best for a particular case.

CLASSICAL DECISION THEORY

According to classical decision theory, decisions should be assigned to the lowest competent level in the organization. This theory is based on the fact that the closer a decision maker is to the problem, the quicker the choice can be made. Also, if too many decisions are passed to higher levels of the organization, the top managers will be overwhelmed and the lower-level managers will have little opportunity to take initiative.

The problem lies in determining the proper level at which a decision should be made. Two factors affecting the level of decision making are the competence of the individual and the level at which all the data necessary to make a fully informed decision can be accessed. Even this distinction may cause a problem, for an individual can make a decision that is best for his or her portion of the organization but which may impact another group. This reality tends to push decisions up the management chain. An example of a decision appearing to impact only one group is the production superintendent's choice to speed up the production line. On the surface, the manufacture of more items per worker hour is desirable. But one hidden factor might be the inspection department's inability to maintain its quality assurance (QA) procedures. This could lead to a lower-quality product and reduced sales. A number of factors can improve a person's decision-making capability, of which the best is experience. Given that it is not logical (or cost-effective) to let a decision maker gain experience by trial and error, the following three courses of action can improve a person's decision-making capability:

1. Train people in decision making. Classroom education may be very cost-effective in the long run, and it will familiarize managers with the conflicting views of experts.

2. Give people in the lower levels of the organization clear-cut authority over particular areas. If this level of responsibility is handled well, more responsibility can be delegated.

3. Use data to convince top management that managers at the lower level are competent decision makers. This may result in greater delegation of responsibility and thus free top managers for policy-making decisions.

DIVERSIONS OF THE DECISION MAKER

Although it would be nice to think that a decision consists of only four factors (the problem, facts related to the problem, uncertainties, and the decision maker), rarely are any of the four clear-cut. There is always the risk that the problem is too broad or complex to be accurately defined. The data, which, we assume, provide us with the facts necessary to make a choice, are themselves subject to error; and more data can always be gathered. The uncertainties may never be clearly understood and, on many occasions, may not even be recognized. But the biggest unknown in any decision-making situation is the actual decision maker. What makes the individual act in a particular way always will be a mystery. In fact, what makes all of us the way we are and act as we do is just as mysterious. We discuss some theories related to this subject in Chapter 4. Here we note some of the diversions that impact the decision-making process.

1. *Prejudice.* The bias may be hidden from the decision maker, who may have some very fixed, yet false, preconceived ideas. For example, the idea that a particular company makes poor- or good-quality products, is late or prompt on delivery, or is dynamic or old fashioned may be a preconceived feeling, received secondhand or through past history, which is no longer true. The idea that a person or an organization is honest or deceptive, smart or dumb, or a good or poor source of data may consciously or subconsciously influence the decisions made. To prevent your being influenced by prejudices, recognize them for what they are and then choose, making a conscious effort not to let these biases influence the quality of your decision.

2. *Showmanship.* Some people are gifted with the ability to "talk a dog off a meat wagon." Usually such an individual is congenial and outgoing, is a born salesperson and everyone's friend. This person also may be able to make a very convincing argument for some point by using slides, movies, handouts, and so on. However, some people are so worried about misleading someone that they present their case in a rather restrained fashion. Still others do not know how to present data in a logical manner, so it is difficult to understand their point. And others go on and on until your mind wanders, and you really do not care what is being said as long as the person stops saying it and goes away. Which person has the best data on which to base your decision? It could be any one. The only way to handle this situation is to note only the facts for the various alternatives. If these people report to you, set a time limit and outline a procedure for presenting the data. If they do not report to you, request that an impartial individual summarize the points made by each source of information.

3. *Analogy.* I once listened to the top man in an organization give an annual "state of the organization" address to the employees. He had an elaborate slide show, which depicted a football team with himself as the quarterback, an army with himself as the general, a horse race with his organization coming in first, and so on. The implication was, "I am the boss; do not question me, and I will give all directions and make all the decisions." Since this organization was very complex and many decisions were made at all levels, this message was false. In fact, the organization ran pretty well, in spite of the lack of specific direction from the top. The danger of analogies is that they may be correct when taken in one way and false when taken in another. The decision maker must separate the implication from the reality. For example, if the boss implies that she or he will make all the decisions, should you wait for the boss before pulling the fire alarm in an emergency?

4. *Transfer.* This diversion is similar to prejudice in that the decision maker may be familiar with a good or bad point regarding a person or an organization and then transfer that feeling. For example, in one highly technical organization, the top manager was a graduate of MIT and truly a brilliant woman. However, her brilliance led to a general acceptance that anyone who graduated from MIT was brilliant. So the entire top-level management team gradually became MIT graduates. Although MIT is an excellent engineering school, it is not the only school that graduates talented engineers. Many highly talented engineers left the organization because merit no longer was viewed as the prime ingredient for success. In another organization, the top man believed strongly moral character to be a highly important factor in a manager. Since he was a Mason and considered himself an excellent example of high moral character, he transferred this feeling to all Masons. Soon it became obvious that anyone who wished to enter the management circle in that particular organization had best be a Mason.

5. *Irrelevant Information.* This problem may be quite common when a choice has to be made between two or more competing ideas or people. One example is a person trying to decide who should be put in charge of a very important research project. The decision maker must be careful not to be distracted by facts irrelevant to the choice at hand. An aide might remind the decision maker that one contender is a sloppy dresser, or that another candidate made mistakes in the past (which is unrelated), or that a third person's spouse is really crude. While this information may be very juicy in the gossip circle, it has no bearing on the selection of the best person for the job, and so it should be ignored.

6. *Facts.* All decision makers love facts, for they are hard and fast data that can be analyzed and compared. However, the facts to be compared must all have the same data base. For example, comparing the prices of two bidders competing for the design and manufacture of a particular item seems straightforward. But do both bids cover overhead? Will the quality of the item be equal for both? Does either bidder have a history of late delivery? Do both use the same material? Are the development and delivery schedules the same? Are both bidders stable? Remember, look deeper than the bottom line to ensure that the costs of equal goods and services are comparable.

7. *Information Source.* Data may be generated inside or outside the organization. Which source should you believe? Neither! In a competitive atmosphere, you will probably not be able to obtain full information on a competitor's success or which line brings in the most profit. If you could obtain this information, you would have an edge over the competition. Even in noncompetitive areas, the facts may be hidden because of the fear of creating competition or the desire to attract investors when additional funds are required. So internal information must be utilized. Will your subordinates provide information that does not support the direction that they believe you favor? Will they present you with data indicating that you (or they) made an error? To combat the various sources of biased data, ask an additional source to research the same information. This individual could be your assistant or secretary, or you could hire two independent sources to obtain the data.

8. *Familiarity.* There is no substitute for experience. This phrase is old, but true in many cases. It is impossible to make an educated decision if you do not understand the circumstances surrounding the problem. In sports, many coaches and managers are ex-players. Think of all the success stories about the boy who started at the bottom of a business and worked his way to the top. He knew the business inside and out, and his broad background enabled him to understand the pros and cons of a decision made at any organizational level. But is this true in all cases? Usually an individual takes a great many years to work up to a position at which the decisions are broad in scope. In these years, things change, not only in the obvious area of technology, but also in many other aspects of the business. For example, the costs in time and money have varied markedly in the marketing distribution area. Management has swung from authoritarian to participatory. Much of the public have become highly educated, environmentally interested buyers. Lessons learned the hard way may no longer apply and may be completely replaced by scientific methodology in lieu of trial and error. Thus you must rely on experts in a particular field. But never rely on them without understanding them. If you cannot understand why an assumption was made when they present their recommendations, then it is possible that the experts don't understand it, either. Imagine one executive's surprise when she asked the marketing man how the sales volume was estimated and he answered that he believed the boss liked the product and any smaller sales volume would have to reflect a loss!

SUMMARY

In this chapter we discussed the decision maker's personal makeup regarding how much risk he or she will be willing to take and how that varies with the commitment required. The higher the risk, the lower the commitment; yet individual preferences vary widely among decision makers. In addition, we discussed the future and limitations of the scientific decision maker, as well as the role of the economic man in this future. Decision makers were categorized according to their reactions in a given situation. Then we talked about the tenet of classical decision theory that a decision should be made at the lowest level possible in the organization, and we explained how this could be implemented. Last, we listed diversions that can influence the decision maker. One of the best ways to avoid these diversions is to be aware of them and to continuously review the decision-making process so as not to fall into one of the many ever-present traps.

Chapter 3

Group Decisions

GROUP PARTICIPANTS

The responsibility for making a decision usually rests with one executive, though it is very rare that he or she actually makes the decision unaided. Even Harry Truman, who had a plaque in his office that read "The Buck Stops Here," was indeed responsible for his decisions; but he did not make those decisions without counsel. In any large organization, the best interests of the organization may appear to be quite clear from one perspective; yet, it is folly to use only that one perspective to make a decision. For example, an increase in sales might appear beneficial from many viewpoints, unless a credit investigation revealed that the increased sales would result in uncollectible accounts receivable. Even the credit investigation was not conducted independently, for information was obtained from banks, personal inquiries, related business activities, and so on.

In the most common method of group decision making, particular tasks are assigned to different elements of the organization. For example, a decision maker can obtain accounting data from the comptroller, legal advice from a lawyer, and technical advice from the engineering department. The successful decision maker must be able to contact the right individual for the information needed. This is not as cut and dry as it may appear, because the right individual is determined by that individual's ability and position in the organization. The wise decision maker tries not only to find out which people have the requisite information, but also to cultivate a personal relationship with them, so that both benefit. Often one finds guidance through the formal chain of command; however, informal contacts and interactions yield the day-to-day information that permits the organization to operate effectively.

One of the best ways to obtain data is by team participation. Instead of asking an accountant for data, you might advise him of the circumstances surrounding the pending decision and get him to provide the appropriate data. The accountant who understands the circumstances surrounding the request may provide the data you really need, and not just the data you think you need (remember, you are probably not an expert in the field of accounting). To make matters worse, without participation, you and the data provider may not even realize that you are requesting and getting data to answer the wrong question.

However, if participation is solicited in decision making, the final decision must be a genuine group decision. If your actions are perceived as being simply a means of manipulating people, trouble is sure to follow. At best, those you try to manipulate will hold you in contempt and may be downright hostile. If people are asked to participate in making a decision, they will believe that it is a measure of respect for their intelligence. If this is true, all is well. If not, then the request will be met with scorn regardless of the actual intent of the decision maker.

SOCIAL SCIENCE

Since few decisions involve only two people, most decisions are made by a group. Thus we are led to the study of social science and what it teaches about group behavior. Studies indicate modern industrial employees follow some well-established principles when it comes to group behavior. The following list itemizes some of these characteristics:

1. If members of a group are able to exchange ideas freely and clearly, they will become involved in the decisions, which results in increased productivity for the group as a whole.

2. A group of capable individuals do not always make a capable group. The reason is related to the fact that the group takes on a personality of its own; and so as it matures, it may develop in a good or bad direction, depending on the situation and members.

3. Groups may be helped to mature in the proper direction. By the use of proper techniques, the efforts of the group can be channeled into effective work, by reducing the internal conflicts that hinder group progress.

4. The ability of the group is not necessarily related to the ability of the group leader. The effectiveness of the group can be improved by a competent leader, but not until group members are willing to accept the responsibility for the way the group acts can it become fully productive.

The social sciences offer some useful guidelines to define an effective group:

1. The group must clearly understand its purpose.
2. The group must be flexible in determining the procedure to be followed to attain its goal.
3. Group members must communicate freely with one another and understand one another's role.
4. Each member must be committed to the major decisions made after all individual viewpoints have been considered.
5. The group must achieve a balance between individual needs and group productivity.
6. There must be a sharing of group leadership so that all alternatives are equally considered.
7. Group members must feel a high degree of pride in such membership.
8. The group must make good use of the various skills of its members.
9. The group should assess its own progress and take corrective action, if necessary.
10. The group should not be dominated by any one member or the leader.

BASIC CONCEPTS OF THE GROUP

As an industrial group works to solve a problem, it is beneficial to understand some of the dynamics within the group. Thus it may be possible to develop a group that is effective in reaching a decision. The basic behavior of the group is impacted by the following factors:

1. *Background.* Every group has a history composed of both its group experiences and the experiences of the group members. A set of values developed as a result of these experiences is transferred to the group's decision-making capability. It is important to perceive the various backgrounds in order to have insight into how the group will react under certain conditions and how well it will function in a given decision-making situation.

2. *Participation.* In a group, people react to one another in many ways. Participation is related to who speaks to whom within the group. A study of these interactions reveals much about the status and power of group members and how well the group utilizes the special talents of

its members. Participation of those group members who can contribute data to the solution of the current problem should be the goal, rather than participation from everyone.

3. *Communication.* This characteristic relates to what people say and how they say it. But we should not limit this factor too strictly to verbal communication, for many other types of communication convey just as much information and sometimes more convincingly, such as facial expressions, gestures, inattention, and so on. Remember that communication is a four-part process: sender, receiver, message, and feedback. This process may be blocked by any of the four not fulfilling its necessary function. The effectiveness of communication can be gaged by such things as the mutual respect of members, the ability to complete the communication cycle, and the presence of positive nonverbal signals.

4. *Cohesion.* This factor relates to the attractiveness the group holds for its members. In business, cohesion is evidenced in the respect that group members show for one another's abilities and contributions to the decision-making process. The benefit of cohesive action is that group members work together to solve a single problem for the good of the organization. If group members feel they can freely contribute to the common goal, for the good of the organization, and put aside personality differences, then they can support the group's decision as if it had been made by any one member alone.

5. *Atmosphere.* If group members feel free to express their ideas freely and are not defensive, a good interchange of viewpoints and ideas can result. This interchange is evidenced by observing individuals express personal feelings and by noting that the group as a whole will support its members. If the atmosphere in which decisions are made is congenial, the group can concentrate on solving the given problem instead of wasting a lot of energy on infighting.

6. *Subgroups.* Subgroups, or cliques, can be beneficial or detrimental in the decision-making process. Cliques may be created as a result of friendship, possibly a common interest, or many other reasons. However, why cliques are formed is not as important as their goals. If the subgroup provides insight into a problem which has not been addressed previously, that is a real service. The trick is not to destroy subgroups, but to direct their efforts to the problem-solving technique.

7. *Standards.* The normal code of operation of the group is its standards. Standards offer a guideline for individual action within the group. For example, do members speak out spontaneously or wait to be called on? The open participation by all members may be extremely beneficial for some decision-making experiences, whereas other discussions may be quite structured. Since standards exist for all groups, it is important to match the pending decision to the proper standard.

8. *Procedures.* To be at all productive, a group should operate within a defined way, to get its work done. Group procedures should be flexible enough to be modified to suit both the particular problem and the size and members of the group. Procedures involve an agenda of events, how discussions are simulated and controlled, and so on. It is vital that all members of the group understand these procedures before proceeding to the problem solving.

9. *Goals.* Goals should be defined as short- or long-term, attainable or unattainable (given the resources of the group), and they must be completely defined and understood by each member. A group with no common goals is like a foot race in which all the runners start off in different directions or a tug-of-war in which half the team pulls one way and the other half pushes the other way.

10. *Leader Behavior.* Although different situations call for either a leader who exercises tight control or one who is led by the group, a good leader will follow the procedure most likely to result in the optimum solution of the problem. Often the leader delegates some leadership functions to group members, so that they share the responsibility of the final decision.

GROUP LEADERS

This final factor brings us back to the key element in utilizing participation in decision making, the responsible group leader. This individual must guide the group decision-making process so that members, while continuously aware of the task confronting them, feel a kinship with other members who are helping solve the problem. The leader achieves this by trying to meet the needs of the group members through soliciting their input. Thus the leader must tend to many task and maintenance functions of the group, such as the following:

1. *Initiating.* This function involves bringing the problem to the attention of the group and suggesting a procedure for finding a solution.
2. *Opinion Seeking.* This task entails seeking relevant information from group members who will not volunteer information unless asked.

3. *Opinion Giving.* A leader should offer personal opinions or any information that may help the group come to a conclusion. However, the leader should not assume the role of dictator.
4. *Clarification.* Occasionally the leader should restate someone else's point, to ensure it is understood by all. This action tends to eliminate confusion resulting from varying interpretations of data presented.
5. *Summarizing.* This function involves pulling together ideas and proposing a decision or conclusion for the group to accept or reject.
6. *Consensus Testing.* The leader continually checks with portions of the group to determine whether progress is being made.

The maintenance functions of a group leader are just as important as the task functions, for these facilitate group members working together to solve a problem rather than going in different directions. Some of the maintenance functions are as follows:

1. *Encouragement.* The leader should be friendly to all group members and show concern for each individual, by giving everyone the opportunity for recognition.
2. *Expression of Group Feeling.* The leader should sense the mood of the group and openly share in it, so that she or he can deal with it appropriately, if necessary.
3. *Harmony.* The leader should try to resolve disagreements among group members. In doing this, he or she should reduce tensions and get people to explore their differences.
4. *Compromise.* The leader whose position or suggestion is threatened should seek a compromise. The leader may have to give in somewhat for the sake of group cohesion.
5. *Gatekeeping.* To keep the lines of communication open, the leader should suggest methods of applying a given member's ideas to solve the problem.
6. *Setting Standards.* A good leader sets the standards for the group. These standards can be used to evaluate the group's progress.

PROBLEMS OF GROUPS

In an industrial organization, it seems reasonable to assume that all people employed by a single firm will work together for the benefit of the firm. And so mutual cooperation will draw people to a combined attack on the problem. However, this is not always the case. Even though all the individuals in a group might benefit by a rapid and effective solution to a problem, certain characteristic problems should be recognized and addressed:

1. *Identity.* When an individual is part of a decision-making group, it may be a frightening and even threatening experience. The individual may ask, "Why am I part of the group? What resources do I have that will be useful toward solving the problem? Am I being tested?" This identity problem affects some people much more than others.

The best way to combat this difficulty is to make sure that the group members' resources are appropriate for the problem at hand and to explain to them why they are members of the group. In addition, there should be a genuine effort to blend talents so that the group operates effectively.

2. *Power and Influence.* Many group members are worried about who the leader will be. Even if there is a clear organizational leader, some members may be concerned that other members will try to increase their influence by demonstrating their leadership talents.

To counter this threat, assign different members of the group leadership functions appropriate to their specialties. For example, the personnel representative should lead the study effort in that area while engineering representatives stick to the technical aspects. This process should be guided by a firm decision-making procedure. Although minority viewpoints should always be considered, the consensus should be clear to all.

3. *Goals and Needs.* There is no guarantee that group members will work together effectively unless the goals of the group and those of the individuals reinforce one another. Both leader and group members must look for and identify the needs of other members. This problem can be difficult to solve when some group members are unaware of their own needs or prefer to hide them.

There is no single solution to this problem. But a concerted effort should be made to integrate group and individual goals by selecting members according to their previous indications. To meet both individual and group needs, the operating procedure should be flexible, so that both organizational and individual goals can be met.

4. *Acceptance.* A member of the group may not feel comfortable about letting his or her needs, difficulties, hopes, and feelings of adequacy or inadequacy be known to other members. Since most organizations are somewhat competitive, it may be very difficult to develop close, trusting relationships among members. One underlying problem is that some members prefer to work alone while others prefer the opposite.

One way to create a feeling of acceptance in all group members is to strive for a balance between communication related to content and to feeling. A genuine freedom to communicate both should prevail. This sense of freedom will be fostered by a tolerance for a wide range of individual behavior. This tolerance should be shown by reacting frankly to an individual's behavior while relating it to the group's purpose.

ADVANTAGES OF A COMMITTEE

1. *Broader Background.* Perhaps the most common reason for using a committee to solve a problem is the fact that a group can bring to bear on a problem a wide range of experience and a variety of opinions on how to solve the problem. Thus facts related to the problem are examined more thoroughly because members with specialized backgrounds tend to ask probing questions in their areas of expertise. If the problem is broad, then the fields associated with the solution cover a larger area than could be covered by the expertise of one individual. This is not to say that only a committee can offer group judgment, because members of a problem-solving team could consult staff specialists; however, advantage would not be taken of the stimulation of face-to-face group communication. Open discussion can lead to the clarification of problems and the development of new ideas. Often a judgment made by a group is superior to that made by a single individual owing to a cross-flow of information and viewpoint.

2. *Spread of Authority.* A committee can be used to solve problems when top management does not wish to delegate too much authority to a single person. This is illustrated by the balance-of-power concept that is the basis of operation of the U.S. government. There is a three-way balance involving the President, Congress, and the Supreme Court. This same concept is witnessed in industry, educational organizations, and even religious organizations. Of the various organizations demonstrating this trait, modern business may be the least notable, perhaps because many businesses started with a single owner-operator who had complete control of the organization. As these organizations grew and the owner-operators passed on, management with decision-making responsibility consulted experts in the various fields related to the firm's operation. In addition, as the organizations became firms administered by boards of directors, the boards were afraid to delegate too much authority to a managing director whose primary connection to the company was financial. This separation of ownership and leadership has given us many leaders who do not wish to take full responsibility for decisions made and who do not trust the advice of a single subordinate.

3. *Special Interest Groups.* Another reason for the growth of committee decision making is the desire for the input of special interest groups. If they are involved, the people who are represented in the decision may support it after it has been made. This practice is particularly appropriate when a portion of the organization (or a member) appears to find fault with every executive decision. By appointing this portion (or member) to participate in finding the solution, it becomes difficult for the portion (or member) to find fault with the final decision. Also, by discussing all aspects of a problem and various potential solutions, a narrow viewpoint may be expanded for the future.

4. *Coordination of Action.* A committee can be an excellent medium for coordinating both the planning and the execution of action required as a result of a decision made. This is very important in a modern organization where the execution of many plans requires that the activities of many departments be integrated. Owing to the large number of specialties in a large organization, this coordination can be quite difficult. The committee permits concerned members to obtain a firsthand picture of the plan and its impact on their portion of the organization. The committee provides a means of making on-the-spot suggestions for implementation of the plan selected and furnishes a structure within which agreement may be reached on the method of implementing needed actions.

5. *Information Exchange.* Information can be effectively exchanged through a committee. The parties affected by a particular action can all learn of its necessity simultaneously. Decisions and instructions can be received uniformly by all parties involved and can be clarified, if required. The time saved by face-to-face discussion may be considerable, and it offers an opportunity for clarification that may not be possible via a written memorandum.

6. *Span of Authority.* On many occasions a decision must be made that is not important enough to be passed up to top-level management but which involves a greater portion of the organization than is controlled by one manager. The decision may be routine but require consolidated action by several departments. The use of a committee permits these departments to consolidate their schedules and actions so that a special effort can be undertaken. An example is a sales department that wishes to get a highly profitable special order, which requires effort by many departments such as engineering, planning, production, materials control, and so on. There is little doubt that the order should be filled. However, a coordinated effort is needed to fill the order without a major disruption to normal operations

7. *Motivation.* Since committees permit wide participation in decision making, they can act as very effective employee motivators. People who take part in a decision usually are enthusiastic about executing it. However, the use of committees to motivate subordinates can be very dangerous. As noted earlier, the solicitation of a committee decision must not be viewed simply as a method to manipulate people, or else more harm than good will ensue.

8. *Avoidance of Action.* At times, managers use committees to avoid action. This is, unfortunately, a very effective way of delaying a decision in the hope that the problem will disappear. By a certain selection of committee members, a delay becomes almost inevitable owing to committee strife, indecisive individuals, or members planted to delay the resolution of the problem. This tactic is a very dangerous procedure. If committee members or an executive in a high-level position feels that a committee was organized as a delay tactic, then the organizer of the committee will have a lot of explaining to do.

DISADVANTAGES OF A COMMITTEE

1. *Cost.* The primary disadvantage of forming a committee is its high cost. In addition to the cost associated with labor hours there may be special travel, lodging, clerical, and space costs. Also the debate over the problem and potential solutions must be aired completely. Thus everyone at the meeting has a right to be heard, and there always seems to be one philosopher on every committee. The exchange of views and clarification of points made are inherent in decisions made by committee and take a lot of time. When an attempt is made to reach a unanimous decision, it takes still longer, if a unanimous decision can be made at all.

2. *Compromise Decisions.* Another disadvantage of a committee-made decision is that a highly dynamic decision is very unlikely. If there are many viewpoints on how to handle a particular problem, then a course of action agreeable to all committee members may well be the least common denominator of the various options. Because it is in the nature of a committee to seek common ground to come to a conclusion, innovative ideas may be discarded rapidly. The reason is that committee members will mostly avoid radical disagreements and accept compromises in order to make a decision acceptable to others.

3. *Failure.* Any committee, despite the high hopes of its members, may find it impossible to agree on a course of action. If the meeting goes on and on and never seems close to conclusion, then the committee may adjourn without deciding on any course of action at all.

4. *Guided Decisions.* When a committee appears to be going in circles and no end is in sight, the chairperson, or senior committee member, tends to push for a conclusion. There can be two reactions. First, the rest of the committee members back off and let the leader make all the decisions. This destroys the committee concept, and only the leader may be fooled into thinking that there is team agreement; all other members of the committee feel railroaded into submission. Second, opposition to the leader's direction develops, and two or more polarized viewpoints emerge. Then many members view themselves in a win-lose position, and so total team support for the chosen course of action is impossible to achieve.

5. *Committee Responsibility.* Another disadvantage of committee decision making is that no one individual is fully responsible for carrying out the final decision because no one individual is fully responsible for making it. The only way to combat this reluctance to complete the necessary actions is to recap those steps which must be taken. This summary should cover who is responsible for specific actions and when they are to be done, and it should be typed up as a conference report and circulated to all involved personnel. Specific actions should be reviewed and agreed to by all committee members before the meeting is adjourned.

6. *Strong Minority.* Just as any member of a committee can take a strong leadership role and destroy the purpose of establishing the committee, so can a minority member. This can occur for example, as a result of a committee's desire to come to a unanimous decision. Say that nine members choose a course of action and the tenth member refuses to agree. What is likely to happen? Would the nine decide to exclude the one dissenter, or would they make some compromise to establish unanimity? Most likely the nine would compromise, even if it is not fully justified. This desire for full agreement can be used very effectively by a minority member as long as the dissent is skillfully disguised as simply a different perspective. The dissenter viewed as bull-headed may find his or her view rejected.

7. *Management Replacement.* Sometimes a committee is formed to replace a lone manager. At times this appears desirable because it eliminates the problem of giving one individual too much authority. However, this eliminates the unified direction that a manager can offer subordinates in accomplishing a task. It would be far wiser to let a committee study a problem and recommend solutions than to let a line manager make the final decision and take the required action. In short, a committee has no place in management, but does have a place in using group thinking to study multifaceted problems.

8. *Research.* A committee should not be used to do research. The answer to a given problem may not be available from any of the committee members, and so the meetings simply waste time. The reason is that research projects are individual efforts, whereas big research projects are coordinated individual efforts. Although the committee meeting may be an excellent method of exchanging data once the research is underway, there is no substitute for the individual's effort and inventiveness.

9. *Trivial Decisions.* Given that decision making by committee is expensive, clearly committee effort should not be expended for the discussion of trivial matters. Since a committee normally is formed by an individual executive, that person must ensure that the cost associated with calling the meeting(s) is proportional to the benefit derived from using committee resources. For example, is committee action necessary to choose carpet colors for a new office space? Only when the colors significantly influence the effectiveness of the personnel moving into the new offices.

10. *Authority.* A committee meeting should never be convened to make decisions that are above the authority of any of its members. This problem can arise when managers send subordinates to represent them at meetings but do not give the subordinates the authority to make binding decisions. One obvious method of eliminating this problem is to make executives either attend the meetings themselves or give the individual representing them the authority to make binding decisions. If this authority is given to subordinates, rarely does the manager have to override the decision made, because the subordinate feels greater responsibility and so strives to do what is right. If a subordinate continually makes poor decisions, then it may be time for a change in subordinates.

SUCCESSFUL GROUP DECISIONS

With all the pros and cons of group decision making, very few managers fail to recognize its value in certain circumstances. The trick is to use group decision making effectively and for the proper decisions. The following are major factors in successful group decisions (to simplify remembering them, they are listed in relation to person, place, and thing):

1. *Person.* Group members should be selected for not only their technical knowledge but also their ability to work together. The combination of group members should bring out the best group thinking, and not in members' ability to compromise. Ideally members should be at approximately equal organizational levels, so that one group cannot dominate another. The group should be kept as small as possible and still have all the skills needed to accomplish the task. The most important aspect of any group decision is selection of the proper leader. The leader must see to it that all the necessary skills are represented and that the effort moves to a logical conclusion.

Once I was on a committee whose task was to combine several technical areas in one system and prepare a report describing the advantages of that system's approach. All the people on the committee strived to push their own areas as most important. So there were lots of meetings, and each time a member tried to put together the system report, it would come out (quite by coincidence) that his technical area filled half the proposed report. Finally, at one of the less productive meetings, I asked the group leader why he did not stop the squabbling among members and get things going toward a conclusion. (I could ask that because I was new in the organization and had no axe to grind.) The leader whispered back to me, "Don't rock the boat!" I am still unsure what he meant, but I recall that the report was never published. If you are the leader and the group is going in circles, by all means *rock the boat* and either adjourn or move toward solving the problem.

2. *Place.* A convenient place and time should be set for all meetings. The time limits associated with meetings and the final decision also should be noted. There is little point in accurately predicting the outcome of an action if it is too late to do anything about it.

I have noted a discouraging increase in the number of meetings in Florida in the winter, or on the opposite coast or in a foreign land. Frequently the justification is that "away" meetings eliminate the day-to-day problems that inevitably call away members of the group. While there may be some slight advantage to being out of telephone's reach, it seems greatly overemphasized. If holding a meeting 3000 miles away from the office is the only way to escape your secretary, then you should hire another secretary. The reason for group decision making is its cost-effectiveness. This measure reflects all costs, even those associated with the decision-making process itself.

3. *Thing.* The thing is the problem. From the start, group members should completely understand their goals and authority. Is the group's function strictly advisory, or should members take action to effect their decision? The task should be so well defined that there is no possibility of different members working in different directions. If there are guidelines for an acceptable range of solutions, this range should be defined. A cost evaluation should be made before the first meeting to assess whether a quick decision process is appropriate at all. If it is proper, then all conclusions should be documented and the people responsible for action identified. A final follow-up meeting should be held to review actions taken and results. This, too, should be documented.

SUMMARY

Clearly very few decisions are made in isolation. The degree and the type of group decision-making process vary with each executive and each problem, but almost all decisions involve more than one person.

Social scientists have provided decision-making guidelines which were ignored in the early days of industry. Some of the characteristics of group behavior were discussed in an effort to show the benefits of group-made decisions. In addition, we listed guidelines to the quality of decision that a group may make.

We examined factors that impact the basic behavior of a group and briefly explained how each factor influences the final decision. Then we considered the functions of group leaders and how these functions could serve the decision-making process.

We talked about problems with group decision making as well as the advantages and disadvantages of committee decisions. We concluded by noting that group decision making is here to stay, regardless of whether we like it or not. Therefore, it is only logical to understand both the strong and weak points of group decision making so we can capitalize on its strong points.

Chapter 4

Human Relations

SOME EARLY HUMAN RELATIONS EFFORTS (TAYLOR, FAYOL, MAYO, AND BARNARD)

Probably no single factor has influenced the methodology of modern industrial decision making more than the human relations movement. This movement did not develop overnight, nor can any individual claim to be the primary catalyst in the study of human relations. One reason is that organizations (of sorts) have existed since the first humans. Two examples are the military and religious organizations that existed in even the oldest or most uncivilized parts of the world. Although it would be stretching a point to claim that human relations as we know it today existed in ancient times, it would be equally foolish to assume that these organizations operated only by chance.

The list of individuals who helped to develop the human relations management philosophy is endless, and a book could be filled with their names and accomplishments. Since the purpose of this text is not to cite history, but to offer some insight and examples on decision making, we discuss a few of the more influencial aspects.

Frederick Winslow Taylor (1856–1915), the father of scientific management, was an engineer who conducted experiments to determine the maximum possible efficiency of workers and machines. He expanded his ideas into a detailed structure for organizing and systematizing factory work. Taylor became known as an efficiency expert. However, his work went far beyond that, for he strived for a complete attitudinal change in both workers and management. He strongly believed that management and labor, working closely together, could create a surplus that would result in increased wages for workers and an equally great increase in profits for manufacturers. Taylor's primary principles of scientific management can be explained as follows:[1]

---

[1]F. Taylor, *Scientific Management*, New York, Harper & Brothers, 1947.

1. Use a scientific approach to determine how work should be done.
2. Foster a group system, rather than individual effort, to accomplish work.
3. Strive for maximum output rather than restricted output.
4. Encourage workers to develop their full potentials for their own good and that of the company.

So what does this have to do with decision making? Directly, nothing. Indirectly, everything. That management should attempt to involve workers in job-related decisions was a radical idea. It necessitated a completely new method of making decisions in an organization.

Another man whom many call the father of modern operational management theory is the French industrialist Henri Fayol. Fayol's work did not appear in the United States until 1949, even though his principles of general management were known in France in 1916. It is mostly for these principles that Fayol is famous:[2]

1. Work should be divided to permit specialization.
2. Authority and responsibility are directly related.
3. Discipline is necessary to enforce agreed-upon behavior.
4. A worker should have only one supervisor.
5. A work group should have one director.
6. Individual interests must be subordinate to general interests.
7. Pay should be fair for work done.
8. Authority should be centralized.
9. A chain of supervision should link top and lower supervisors.
10. People and things should be in a logical order.
11. Employee loyalty should match management justice.
12. Turnover should be minimized with tenure provided to employees.
13. Managers should allow subordinates to take initiative.
14. Good communication should foster an esprit de corps.

To the modern manager, these principles may appear to be nothing more than common sense. Yet common sense is developed from background experiences that have been accepted as logical according to current social customs. If it is a social standard that the organization owner's word is law, then any suggestion that the workers' views be considered is certainly radical.

---

[2]H. Fayol, *General and Industrial Administration*, London, Sir Isaac Pitman & Sons, Ltd., 1949.

One of the most significant contributions to modern decision making involved an experiment whose results were so surprising that the researchers were forced to reassess the importance of involving employees in group decision making. We refer to the famous "Hawthorne experiments" conducted by Elton Mayo, F. J. Roethlisberger, and others at a Western Electric Company from 1927 to 1932.[3] The experiment was set up primarily to determine the effect of illumination on workers' productivity. The idea was to vary the illumination of a test set of employees and to record their productivity. The workers were assigned rather tedious work, and researchers expected the efficiency of the test group to drop as the illumination was reduced. One goal was to determine the minimum amount of illumination needed for workers to perform at an acceptable level. By knowing this level, employers could minimize costs. The results were that productivity went up as illumination went down and productivity went up as illumination went up. Regardless of what the experimenters did, productivity increased. In fact, changing illumination, modifying rest periods, shortening the workweek, and developing various incentive pay schemes had no correlatable impact on the work group.

Obviously, some factor was being overlooked. Mayo and colleagues concluded that the most significant effect on productivity resulted from the separation of the test group from the rest of the workforce. This group developed a social attitude and pride in being a part of the experiment, which greatly enhanced their output. This experiment led to the development of the understanding of group behavior which radically changed older ideas of the proper procedure for effective management. Clearly a business is not a collection of machines operated by faceless robots. A business is a social system in which various personalities interact. This interface may be to the benefit or detriment of the business itself. This realization did a great deal toward emphasizing the human relations aspects of business and the improved decision-making process that can be developed by recognizing the importance of this social system.

Chester I. Barnard is another man who significantly influenced modern decision making and leadership. He was what might be called a practicing executive, the president of the New Jersey Bell Telephone Company from 1927 to 1948. Barnard studied the tasks of a manager

[3]E. Mayo, *The Human Problems of an Industrial Civilization*, New York, The Macmillan Company, 1933.

and how they fit in with the business social system. The logic of his approach is outlined as follows:[4]

1. Physical and biological limitations of individuals lead people into a group effort with supportive cooperation.
2. This cooperation leads to the development of a cooperative system which would move toward a single purpose.
3. This cooperative system may be divided into two parts: *organization* (this is the "people" system) and *other elements*.
4. The organizational element can be subdivided into *formal* and *informal*, with formal being the structured portion of the organization and informal being the uncoordinated part of the organization.
5. The formal organization utilizes a set communication system, combines effort by group action, and has a conscious single purpose.
6. Each formal organization must have a system for specialization, a system of incentives for group actions, a system of authority (so group members will accept the decisions of executives), and a system of logical decision making.
7. The formal functions of the executive are to maintain communication within the organization, to secure services for members of the organization, and to plan for the group's goals.
8. The executive balances conflicting forces and events to move the organization towards its goal.
9. To be effective, the executive must lead organization members by using cooperation.

This brief review of four of the most influential scholars from the mid-1800s to the mid-1900s indicates the early trend in modern management. The theories set forth by these pacesetters and many others are still considered valid.

SOME MODERN HUMAN RELATIONS EFFORTS (McGREGOR, MASLOW, AND HARRIS)

One of the most famous modern behavioral scientists is Douglas McGregor. In his book[5] he set forth the concept that two assumptions

[4]C. I. Barnard, *The Functions of the Executive*, Cambridge, Mass., Harvard University Press, 1938.

[5]D. McGregor, *The Human Side of Enterprise*, New York, McGraw-Hill Book Company, 1960.

can be made about employees in an organization. The first is based on the thinking of an autocratic manager and is called *theory X*. The second, based on the thinking of a permissive manager, is referred to as *theory Y*. Although the theory X and theory Y concepts are based on absolutely no research, it is interesting to note the wide acceptance they have enjoyed. The reason may be the simplicity of the concept and the ability of most people to relate to an individual who falls into one or the other category.

Theory X managers make the following assumptions about their employees:

1. The average human dislikes work and avoids it if possible.
2. Because of this dislike for work, most employees must be coerced, controlled, directed, and threatened to get them to work toward an organizational objective.
3. The average employee prefers to be directed, wishes to avoid responsibility, has little ambition, and wants security above all.

At the opposite extreme, the theory Y manager is said to assume the following:

1. The expenditure of physical and mental effort at work is as natural as play or rest.
2. External control and threats are not necessary if employees are committed to organizational objectives. They will exercise self-direction and self-control.
3. Commitment to objectives is a function of the rewards associated with their achievement.
4. Under proper conditions, the average human being not only accepts, but also seeks responsibility.
5. The capacity to exercise imagination, ingenuity, and creativity in solving organizational problems is widely distributed among employees.
6. In modern industrial life, the intellectual potential of the average employee is only partially utilized.

This theory provoked follow-up analyses by a number of behavioral scientists. Even though all have modified McGregor's concept (one added a theory Z, which combines the best of both worlds), they all emphasize the need for managers to match their management style to the given problem and to the people available to solve it.

Psychologist Abraham Maslow developed a theory about motivation which is widely used to illustrate the needs of individuals.[6] Although his identification of need is not accepted by all, it (like McGregor's work) caused people to come up with a number of studies and theories about employee needs and their reality or unreality. Maslow theorized that employees in an organization have basic needs and that these needs are related—unless a lower need is met, the individual is not interested in striving to meet a higher need. This is very interesting with respect to decision making. If this is true, it would be a waste of time to attempt to interest employees in solving a problem related to a higher-level need if they are preoccupied with a lower-level need. These are the basic human needs as identified by Maslow:

1. *Physiological Need.* This need encompasses the basics for sustaining life, such as food, water, clothing, shelter, sleep. If this need is not met, Maslow believes, no other motivator will affect the decision-making process. For the purposes of an organization, this need can be met by offering a high enough salary for the individual to have an acceptable personal life.

2. *Security, or Safety.* This factor involves the need to be free from physical danger or the fear of loss of a job, property, food, and so on. This need of employees can be met, on the job, by offering them job security and safe working conditions. High-quality supervision, which is essential for both this need and need 3, can help employees feel like needed members of the organization.

3. *Affiliation, or Acceptance.* People are social beings who need to be accepted by others. Both the formal and informal interpersonal relationships developed in an organization help fulfill this need. Company policy and administration have a strong influence. For example, a significant reduction in workforce affects more than simply the personnel being discharged.

4. *Esteem.* Maslow believes that the individual who has satisfied the need to belong will want to be held in esteem by coworkers and himself. This need is met in an organization by providing prestige, status, advancement, recognition, and so forth.

5. *Self-actualization.* This need to become or do the best that one can is the highest need of the five. Individuals want to maximize their potentials in the accomplishment of a task. Employees should be given chal-

---

[6]A. Maslow, *Motivation and Personality*, New York, Harper & Row, Publishers, Incorporated, 1954.

lenging work and potential job advancement, which relate to increased responsibilities and achievement.

The hierarchy of needs, although interesting, is very difficult to use in practice. However, keep in mind that when a problem is reviewed in an organization, the decision makers seeking a solution will have more than simply organizational achievements in mind. Depending on the level of needs involved in the decision-making process, the individual's behavior may be influenced by personal needs. Thus it would plainly be a mistake to have individuals work on long-range organizational goals who were afraid of losing their jobs; or to put an egotist (who wants an office about the size of Yankee Stadium) in charge of making decisions regarding an office layout where he will be working.

A book written by Dr. Thomas A. Harris has attracted considerable attention in behavioral science.[7] The success of the concept proposed in this book (and one reason for its national favor) is due to the simplicity of its rationale. Basically, Harris stripped away the technical language of psychoanalysis and presented a logical method of self-understanding. He developed a way for people to understand how the mind operates and why we do the things we do.

Harris calls this process of self-understanding *transactional analysis.* Currently it is used in group therapy, marital counseling, treatment of adolescents, pastoral counseling, and many business courses related to human interfacing. One reason for its success is that transactional analysis works best in groups, because it is a tool to understand why people act as they do.

The basic concept of transactional analysis is that every personality is split into three parts: the parent, the adult, and the child. The parent (P) portion is composed of the events perceived by a person from birth to age 5, such as actions that we observed our parents (or parent substitutes) take. The adult (A) portion of the personality differs from the parent portion (which is judgmental) in that it acts on pieces of information and reacts through exploration and testing. The child (C) portion reacts to events mostly as a result of internal feelings.

Here are some statements typical of the separate portions of the personality:

MOTHER (P): Go pick up your room.

DAUGHTER (C): You cannot tell me what to do. You are not the boss.

[7]T. A. Harris, *I'm O.K.—You're O.K.*, New York, Avon Book Division, The Hearst Corporation, 1969.

THERAPIST (A): What is your main hang-up in life?

PATIENT (C): (Pounding the table) Red tape, damn it, red tape!

SON (A): I have to finish a report that is due tomorrow.

MOTHER (P): Why do you always leave things until the last minute?

LITTLE GIRL (C): I hate soup. I am not going to eat it. You cook icky.

FATHER (C): I am going to leave, and then you can cook your own icky food.

These examples show that there is no set age at which any one of the three personality traits dominates. In fact, anyone can exhibit various portions at different times. The idea is that an adult-to-adult relationship must exist for there to be a meaningful exchange of information. This concept demonstrates how difficult it would be to make a group decision if some members let other than the logical portions of their personalities prevail.

According to Harris, if an adult-to-adult relationship exists, then both members of the exchange will recognize this fact and both will feel O.K. If one reacts as a parent or a child, then the signal is sent that the other person is not O.K., and so the communication process deteriorates.

SOME VISUAL CONCEPTS OF HUMAN RELATIONS

One recent trend is to provide managers with graphic illustrations to explain what may be vague concepts. Here we present some exercises designed to draw attention to the concepts described.

These two exercises illustrate the limitation inherent in decision makers who view a problem from their perspectives only. Figure 7 shows a

Figure 7   Dot-limited perception problem.

set of points in a geometric pattern. Try to connect the dots with four straight lines such that the end of one line is the start of another and the four lines together go through all the dots. Can it be done?

The second exercise is similar to that of Figure 7 in that it also tests an individual's perception. The task is simply to count the number of square blocks represented by Figure 8.

Figures 7 and 8 both fall into the category of games. However, neither has any trick to it. Both simply illustrate (graphically) how we can be limited in our perspective until we view a problem without the limitations that we impose on ourselves. This exercise illustrates the benefit of attacking a problem by group collaboration.

Figure 8   Block-limited perception problem.

Many people would find it impossible to solve the problem in Figure 7. The difficulty lies not in the restrictions outlined by the problem, but in the self-imposed requirement that all the straight lines remain within the block outlined by the geometric pattern or the dots. Once it is clear that this limitation does not exist, the solution is much easier to find. Often we impose similar limitations on ourselves unknowingly when we attempt to solve a problem.

I once knew of an executive who had to fill a middle management position. Company policy was to fill all administrative positions from within the organization. However, when the executive reviewed the potential candidates, he found serious drawbacks in all. He pondered and made elaborate lists of pros and cons for each candidate. Valuable time went by without a selection being made. Finally, the supervisor asked why the executive had not filled the vacant position. When he explained that he could not support any of the candidates, the supervisor's immediate response was, "If you cannot promote from within, why not advertise the position?" It was also company policy to promote only highly qualified individuals. This dialogue opened up a whole new world of candidates. Then the problem was to choose the most likely to succeed from a significant number of highly qualified applicants. Figure 9, the solution to the problem posed in Figure 7, shows the advantage of not restricting one's thinking when one is trying to solve a problem.

The problem in Figure 8 has a different message. On occasion, we may not recognize the resources available within the organization. We may think we recognize the talents within the organization, but do we? It is impossible for executives to know all the talents available to them; likewise, sometimes we cannot identify all an executive's talents and

Figure 9   Solution to dot-limited perception problem.

capabilities. Often, there is a difference between what we can do and what we are sure we can do simply because we have not been suffi-ciently challenged to develop our capabilities. The same is true of many people hidden behind domineering supervisors: they may have never been really challenged. To return to the previous example, did all the potential candidates have serious drawbacks, or were these drawbacks simply the result of the candidates having lacked the opportunity to demonstrate their capabilities? This judgment may be one of your more difficult decisions—should you consider a trial promotion? In any event, the solution to the problem in Figure 8 is 30 blocks. Figure 10 shows how to find the proper number of blocks.

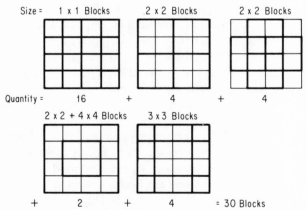

Figure 10   Solution to block-limited perception problem.

LEARNING

Once Senator Robert Kennedy stated, "Good judgement is usually the result of experience; and experience is usually the result of bad judge-ment." Good decision-making judgment in human relations is strongly related to learning experience. Learning experience can be gained best by making poor decisions. In Figure 11 an abstract cone is divided into three passive and four active learning activities. The cone reflects the intensity at which the decision-making experience is beneficial to future decision-making events.

The order of benefit from studying decision making is indirectly related to the level of abstraction. Thus reading this book is only one

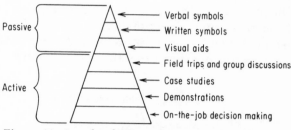

Figure 11   Levels of Abstraction in learning.

level better than verbal instructions related to decision making. The best method of improving decision-making capability is by on-the-job decision making. This is also the most expensive method in relation to the cost of poor decisions. It is difficult to improve the decision-making capability because often an entirely new behavioral change is required after the process of decision making has been learned. This required change induces a fear of the unknown. It is much easier to do things as they always have been done than to examine alternatives. However, the purpose of learning is growth in a behavioral change. This growth results in an overall improved decision-making capability.

Seven conditions must be met to create a successful learning situation:

1. The learner must bring to the transaction needs and ability, as well as ignorance of the decision-making process.
2. The teacher must bring a knowledge of the decision-making process to the transaction.
3. There must be a proper setting in which the learning and change take place.
4. There must be an interaction process.
5. Both mental and physical conditions necessary for learning must be correct.

6. The learning function must result in the maintenance of the changes developed.

7. The learning process must include a continual process for additional learning.

JOHARI WINDOW

One illustration that may help an executive visualize the problems to be faced in a joint decision-making process with someone else is the *Johari window*. This concept uses a block diagram like the window in Figure 12. This concept shows that there are two portions to each person's abil-

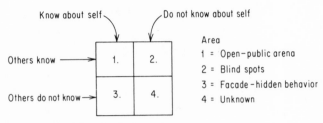

Figure 12 Johari window.

ity, personality, experience, and so on, which are partially known and partially unknown to the person. There exist also an area that is seen by others and an area that is not. The area which we know about ourselves and which others know about us is the open, or public, area, where we can work with other people. It is in this area that we can interfere with others in making a group decision.

By recognizing the four areas associated with any interpersonal relationship, hopefully we can act to increase the open area. To learn more about ourselves, we must get feedback from our actions. To increase the size of the area in the other direction, we simply must be more open in exposing our true selves.

Note that when two people interact, the Johari window for one of them may not be the same as that for the other person in the interaction. In the combined open area, they can work on the given problem. When one or both people hold back information, the open area gets smaller and decision making becomes more difficult. Also an individual's Johari window may vary depending on the person with whom he interacts. Figure 13 illustrates these primary tendencies:

1. Subordinates may know little about you.
2. You and your family know you very well.
3. Your boss may know more about you than you think.
4. You and your spouse know each other well.
5. You do not know what coworkers know about you.
6. You know your own capabilities in a particular class, but your classmates do not.

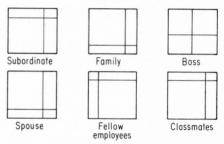

Subordinate   Family   Boss

Spouse   Fellow employees   Classmates

Figure 13   Typical Johari windows.

SUMMARY

In this chapter we only touched on some of the social science work regarding industrial human relations. Both the early and modern examples were typical of the work that has influenced and changed decision making in modern industry.

At the turn of the century, Taylor revealed some of the first, if not most important, changes necessary in industry. Would these changes have occurred anyway, without these pioneers? Probably. The average employee was becoming more intelligent and more mobile in job selection. This change in the working class was not unique to the United States. Fayol was making similar discoveries and outlining new management principles in Europe at approximately the same time as Taylor. Mayo's Hawthorne experiment was one of the first industrial experiments to validate both Taylor's and Fayol's concepts. We discussed Barnard to show that management theory is not confined to social scientists, but also is studied and enlarged by practicing managers.

Modern management practices and theories have developed via evolution, not revolution. However, once the concepts had been created, many modern industrial psychologists turned their attention from what the modern rules of management should be to why they should be what they are. As a result, a number of theories emerged in the attempt to simplify and explain human behavior. The theories of McGregor, Maslow, and Harris are only a sampling of the concepts that have been developed. None of the theories have been universally accepted as true, but they have not been dismissed as having no validity.

In addition to examples of early and modern writers we illustrated graphically some concepts that may be abstract with only verbal explanation. We briefly explained learning abstraction and a concept related to interpersonal relationships.

Our purpose in this chapter was not so much to provide complete information, but rather to underline the tremendous amount of work done in human relations and its impact on organizational decision making. Never has the saying "No man is an island" been so true in relation to executive decisions as today.

Chapter **5**

Nonmathematical Decision-Making Techniques

INTRODUCTION

Decision making involves the gathering of facts, and various techniques can be used to obtain information pertaining to a given problem. Another technique is to consult experts in the field and to draw on their decision-making experience. Both methods reflect the bias of the individual decision maker. This bias is related to the principle that in any decision two premises influence the final outcome. The first premise is the value of the decision as perceived by the decision maker. The second is the acceptance of certain information as fact. However, the information may or may not be fact, for the decision maker's viewpoint will affect what he or she perceives to be facts. Thus fact-finding techniques have become very popular and helpful in solving certain types of problems. The following represent some common techniques.

BRAINSTORMING

Brainstorming is one of the oldest methods of gathering data about a particular problem. It was first used widely by the military, and ever since it has been employed throughout industry. Brainstorming is most effective in generating new ideas.

Normally a group of people interested in solving a particular problem is assembled. This technique is best performed in a classroom, where the problem or question can be written on the chalkboard for all to see. The leader explains the problem and the rules of the exercise, such as the following:

1. Rule out all judgments. No idea should be criticized or evaluated in any way before all ideas relevant to the problem are considered.
2. Welcome wild ideas. The wilder the idea, the better. It is always easy to tame down or discard ideas, but it may be very difficult to generate them.
3. Strive for quantity, not quality. The more ideas there are, the more likely a good one will come up.
4. Look for combinations and improvements. By encouraging participants to add to or modify other participants' suggestions, the system can make improvements not visualized by the original suggestor.

Next the leader asks two or more people to record the suggestions in plain sight on the chalkboard, so that participants can see the proposed ideas and build on them. The leader should specify who is to record a particular idea, so the group does not have to wait for one idea to be recorded before a second can be identified and recorded.

Usually ideas emerge slowly at first; then the tempo picks up rapidly just prior to a slow decline. This can be the result of one person proposing an offbeat idea and someone else quickly trying to top it. A third person may come up with an even stranger idea, but one that can be used to modify the first two. Often this exchange is contagious, and the ideas come fast and furious. While no single idea may be worthwhile, the combination of two or three may produce a thought that no individual would have imagined alone.

A single session can easily produce over 100 ideas, but many will be impractical. A few will be worthy of serious consideration. To separate the ideas to be discarded from those to be evaluated further, sort them into categories. Then many ideas can be combined and others eliminated.

Brainstorming is most effective when the problem is simply stated and specific. This procedure is time-consuming and can therefore be very expensive. Both the session itself and the follow-up sorting and evaluation are very time-consuming. A complex problem should be broken down into parts for evaluation, and each part should be clearly defined in order to eliminate ideas which do not apply. It is also possible that all the ideas will be worthless. Yet the process is still quite popular, for many managers believe that people get involved in decision making and the stimulation carries over to other company activities. These managers feel that the wasted time associated with brainstorming can be minimized by choosing group members who have an interest in and understanding of the problem.

SYNECTICS

A modern method of generating data and ideas through group activity is *synectics*. It is similar to brainstorming in that it is based on the same principle—that all people possess a certain creativity. The process is designed to elicit these creative ideas and to use them for problem solving. Like brainstorming, synectics attempts to gather apparently emotional, or irrational, ideas and combine them with the rational elements of decision making. The final solution to the problem is found by a methodology that is similar to but more structured than brainstorming.

These are the basic steps of synectics:

1. The problem is studied thoroughly. This step involves a highly technical review of all aspects of the problem, both in detail and in broad terms. All group members must become thoroughly familiar with the nature and limitations of the problem before any attempt is made to find or suggest a solution.

2. The leader selects a key portion of the problem, which is used for this segment of problem analysis.

3. Group members employ various means to inspire ideas about this portion of the problem. These devices may be symbolic analogies or other techniques proven to be useful in developing novel ideas and viewpoints. Each group member must be aware of the purpose of these devices and therefore cooperate in their development.

4. The group skilled in this process can vacillate between an irrelevant discussion and the real problem. There must be at least one technical expert in the group to evaluate the feasibility of ideas and to discard the infeasible ones.

Synectics has both strong and weak features. The positive side is that random ideas and thoughts are discarded immediately. Therefore, the analysis portion associated with brainstorming is reduced in scope. Also since the problem is attacked in segments, a much more complex problem can be evaluated systematically. The negative side is twofold: the group will need training to utilize devices such as symbolic analogies, and technical "experts" may reject ideas of little apparent merit which, in reality, are simply unfamiliar to them.

CONSENSUS THINKING

When knowledge of a particular issue is spread among several people, many experts feel that consensus thinking is the best way to use this combined knowledge. Figure 14 shows how experts assess the effectiveness of various decision-making techniques.

Various researchers have evaluated the results of groups who use this technique and compared them with those of experts in the given field. This comparison has been favorable in most respects. The steps

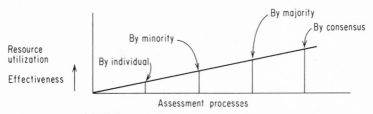

Figure 14 Effectiveness assessment of concensus decision-making.

involved in consensus thinking are similar to those used in synectics. The main advantage of the consensus approach is twofold: group members do not have to be skilled in such things as symbolic analogies, and consensus decisions do not require total agreement by all group members. Nonetheless, the decision should be generally acceptable to everyone; if it is not, then not all inputs have been considered completely and more discussion is in order. A consensus decision is reached as follows:

1. Define the problem in terms that are specific and reasonably acceptable to group members.
2. All group members pool their information regarding the problem. Everyone's input must be included, so all group members start with the same data base.
3. Develop a model to encompass the pooled information.
4. The group tests whether the model is applicable to the given problem.

There is nothing particularly unique about these steps; they are the same steps that an individual would take to solve the problem alone. What is different is that forcing a group to follow the same procedure reduces much of the time needed to make a decision. Time is saved by preventing individuals from jumping to step 4 before completing the necessary groundwork. Often this tendency to jump to conclusions causes group members to push for their own solutions with a win-lose attitude; yet they may not even have a common understanding of the problem. As well as rigidly holding to the four-step procedure, group members should follow these suggestions carefully:

1. Avoid arguing for one's own position.
2. Do not get trapped into the win-lose syndrome.
3. Do not change positions simply to reach agreement, except when the evidence justifies the switch.
4. Avoid simplistic solutions, such as coin flipping, that only end the debate.
5. Elicit differences in opinion, because new light may be shed on a subject.
6. Present information as clearly and objectively as possible.
7. Strive to keep a positive attitude toward the group's ability to solve the problem.

Proponents of consensus thinking claim that it not only makes maximum use of talents available, but also commits group members to follow the action they choose. If so, the strength of this tool may reach far beyond the single problem studied. And any system of group decision making that avoids disagreement among group members is worth trying.

DELPHI TECHNIQUE

The Delphi technique is a method of predicting the future by using experts in the problem area. Typically a group of experts in a particular field is assembled, and they independently predict future events. Follow-up questions might touch on the possible occurrence of the event, its desirability, and its significance.

A series of questions related to individuals' areas of expertise are distributed to each member. One possible use is to question the management of an organization about its estimates of future markets or products. Another example is a group of career government employees who are asked questions about the goals of the Department of Defense. Group members could be asked to predict exactly when certain events would occur. Individuals could check off blocks of time of 5, 10, 15, 20 years later, or never. Another block could show the individual's judgment of the goal: of high desirability, of medium desirability, of low desirability, of low undesirability, of medium undesirability, or of high undesirability. The last block could reflect the individual's estimate of this goal's impact on the quality of a given service. This category could comprise very great, great, moderate, and no impact. The last column is for remarks. Group members should be told to check only one block in each of the three categories.

Questions about the goals of the Department of Defense might cover items such as full integration of women into all facets of military service, reduction of expenditures to 20 percent of the federal budget, elimination of all educational qualifications for entry into military service, and so on.

The questionnaires are then collected and reviewed. The next day a follow-up questionnaire is returned that shows each individual's previous answers. The group median consensus is found also. This questionnaire could contain a space to indicate revised judgments (by marking an X in the appropriate column), even though an individual's second choice may not be different from the first one. If an individual's choice is different from the median, a brief explanation is requested. All the questionnaires are coded so that individuals know only their own and the group's position, thus preventing direct conflict between individuals.

Following the second questionnaire, a third and final set of judgments is recorded, including group medians from the second questionnaire and the reasons given for earlier judgments that deviated from the group median. If such reasons are extensive, the group leader could ask group members to go over the items one at a time and verbally describe their reasons for varying from the norm. All this should be accomplished without direct interaction among group members. A final set of judgments is marked in the appropriate column, and again reasons for deviations from the median are given.

This exercise yields a data bank of expert opinions on every question asked. Also the decision maker who analyzes these knows the median response to various questions by experts in the field. All this can be done with no direct conflict among individuals in the group and therefore a minimum of time is lost in gathering opinions. Those disagreements that do arise are well documented as to why opinions vary from the norm. The disadvantage of this technique is its inability to treat problems requiring more answers than can be categorized by check columns. In addition, individual brilliant ideas might be cast off by a group member in an attempt to join the norm. The disadvantage associated with the rare selection of a radical course of action which may be highly successful is common to most group decision-making procedures.

FISHBOWLING

The word *fishbowling* refers to a technique in which the decision-making group is seated in a circle. In the center is a single chair. When someone is seated in the center chair, only the individual in that chair may speak. Thus the attention of group members is forcibly directed to the person in the center. The person in the center seat can present, unopposed, his or her views and propose solutions to the given problem. This procedure eliminates cross-talk and irrelevant discussion. With a single chair in the center position, two techniques can be used.

First, a spokesperson with expertise in the area of discussion is invited to sit in the fishbowl. The center expresses personal views on the subject and explains how to handle the problem. Group members may ask the center questions, but they may not speak to any other member. Once this person's viewpoint is fully understood, he or she leaves. A second expert is called upon, follows the same procedure, and then leaves. The number of experts who can sit in the fishbowl is limitless. Also there is no rule prohibiting group members from using information gained from previous experts to question subsequent experts. This system results in each group member favoring, individually, one course of action. After the experts have testified and the group works to choose a course of action, this becomes evident. Theoretically this happens because each member is acting in accordance with the same data base.

Second, a group of decision makers is gathered, as before, but it consists of experts only (no outside assistance is required). A single leader sits in the center chair and explains the rules and the problem. The leader may even propose a solution. Then the leader gets up and joins the group in the circle of chairs. There may be a long delay at this point, because no one can start a discussion without taking the center chair. The second person to move into the fishbowl offers a solution, modifies the previous discussion, or recommends that the previous solution be accepted. The second person may not suggest that his or her particular solution be accepted. Exchange between the center chair and group members continues until the chair is vacated.

At times, frustration may set in, for two group members may wish to talk directly, which is against the rules. To make matters worse, the person in the center may not relinquish the position before believing the point has been adequately established. Occasionally, group members suggest that the center position be relinquished. This exercise is concluded when someone sits in in the center and recommends adoption of a previous speaker's suggestion. A majority show of hands in favor of the recommendation ends the session. Although it might seem simple to get a majority to agree, it is not. The reason is that neither those members who favor another, different solution nor those members who are undecided or who wish to discuss aspects of the proposed solution in greater depth will vote for the recommendation.

A third variation of the single-chair fishbowl technique involves making group discussions manageable. Many times a large group is counterproductive in decision making, simply because of the time required to hear all viewpoints and the number of viewpoints that may differ in minor points only. Many feel that the best size for a group discussion is five people, six maximum. Various factions appoint a single representative to represent their views. The fishbowl consists of a small group of representatives from the larger group who sit in a circle and interact while the larger group looks on. Members of the larger group are included in the decision process and fact finding, but only through the group representative. This is possible because members of the large group sit close to and have access to their representative. This system is a good means of reporting information quickly, encouraging interaction, clarifying points, and making the whole group aware of all aspects of the problem and solution, by listening to other representatives explain their viewpoints.

DIDACTIC INTERACTION

Didactic interaction is a procedure that is not used often because it is appropriate in certain situations only. However, when these situations arise, it is an excellent problem-solving technique.

The problem must require a go–no go type of decision, such as to buy or not, to sell or not, to merge or not, and so forth. The factors related to the final decision may be extremely complex and their investigation quite broad. To obtain a concentrated effort in a decision, assign one group or person to list all the pros of the problem and a second to list all the cons. After a reasonable time the two sides meet and discuss the findings. Following this meeting, the researchers switch sides. In a second meeting participants find holes in their own original arguments. Through this interchange mutually accepted facts can be presented and used to solve the problem, and a final decision can be readied.

A secondary use of the basic concept occurs when two or more factions are polarized in relation to a certain problem and cannot agree. Each faction is directed to support the opposite position. The first reaction will be that this exchange cannot be accomplished. But after a time, participants realize that the other position has some good points. When both sides build on the good points of the position assigned, often mutually agreeable ground can be found. If common ground is not found, there may be a deeper problem. The people involved may be forgetting that the rational decision maker tries to maximize desirable consequences and minimize undesirable ones. The identification in an organization of someone as a person who cannot find any merit in another's viewpoint could easily cause others in the organization to view that person as an individual with whom they cannot work. An example of an area where this technique could be used is when two marketing managers disagree over the extent of their areas or two department heads dispute their areas of responsibility. The possibility of the switch in position becoming permanent could add a sense of reality to the arguments developed.

COLLECTIVE BARGAINING

Collective bargaining is unique in that it uses conflicting viewpoints rather than a single concentrated effort to solve a problem. In many cases this type of decision making can be categorized as a *zero-sum interaction*. This means that anything you win is at my expense. The attitude is bound to influence the decision maker's approach to and solution of the problem.

Collective bargaining usually is a result of labor coming to management for negotiation. When the opposing sides meet, they approach the table with a strategy. The strategy involves a list of items desired and a backup position for each item. If the backup positions overlap, agreement can be reached finally. If not, agreement is impossible.

One major problem is the distrust of each party for the other. Unfortunately this distrust is often justified, for both sides take diverse, yet differing positions in an effort to give the impression of having made the final offer. Both parties recognize these positions as a façade.

To come to an agreement within a reasonable time, it is recommended that the parties enter into *constraint bargaining*, in which both sides put limits on the bargaining concession before it starts. Commonly both sides list items believed to be mutually agreeable, say, place and time of negotiation and items to be discussed. The idea is that the more constraints are placed at the beginning, the more likely a decision will be reached in a short time.

The method that I believe has the best chance of stimulating a successful collective bargaining session is called the *needs theory*. It is a workable approach which has been successful in practice. According to the approach of needs theory, one month early, each side defines the problems to be discussed at the bargaining table. Then for each problem each side makes three proposals and explains how they meet both parties' needs. Chances are that at least one proposal from each side will be similar to that from the other side. And since the needs of both parties must be delineated, lopsided proposals tend to be dismissed before ever getting to the table. Negotiation should continue for no more than a week. If agreement has not been reached in that time, further delays only tend to polarize positions. The final decision must be handled by an impartial arbitrator when agreement cannot be reached.

RATIONAL AND NEGOTIATED DECISION MAKING

The rational decision-making process involves growing awareness of and identification of the problem, determination of who and what are involved and whether a solution is possible, identification of alternatives and their probable and possible consequences, selection of the best solution, implementation of the decision, and collection of feedback. This decision-making loop is not static; it depends to a great extent on the organizational environment of the individual decision.

Negotiation forces confrontation among individuals or teams with preconceived and conflicting ideas, but provides no system for its resolution. Consequently, negotiators wishing to avoid the consequences of failure must find a way to resolve their differences by mutual adjustment. The discussion may range from rational, cooperative problem solving to persuasion to cajolery and threats.

The most publicized form of negotiation is collective bargaining. There are three recognized methods of effecting a settlement by talking:

1. Threatening force or violence
2. Invoking the assistance of a third party
3. Persuading, compromising, and integrating

The third method may employ the rational decision-making process. Each party should take every opportunity to make the other realize that he or she is being understood. A party accomplishes this by seeking areas of mutual ground and reinforcing every sign that the opponent is heard and understood. If it is successful, a two-way flow of understanding may open the way to agreement.

In negotiation, one must leave a way for the opponent to change position without losing face. For this reason, there is a place in negotiation for ambiguity of claim and statement, something highly undesirable in ordinary communication. Ambiguous statements can be explained or redefined with changes in circumstance, providing room to maneuver, to change position, and to save face if necessary.

The primary difference between rational decision making and decision making through negotiation is not the process. Rather, negotiations involve two sides with different frames of reference. Therefore, their solutions most likely will not be compatible. In fact, the definitions of the problem itself may vary. However, if both sides follow rational decision-making procedures and utilize the need theory, they can find common ground. This is possible because both sides have overlapping backup positions, enabling space for mutual agreement. This process can be expedited if both sides agree about the premise of what is fact before attempting to settle the value conflict. It is as though both sides said, "I respect your right to disagree, but not your right to be wrong."

SUMMARY

Recent trends in decision making have tended more and more toward quantitative analysis. Although this may be a positive step in many cases, quantitative analysis will never completely replace the human element, which provides the irreplaceable quality of judgment that cannot be defined mathematically. Quantitative techniques cannot be used to solve a problem until a human being feeds the proper data into the computations.

In this chapter we discussed nonmathematical techniques to gather data or to solve a given problem. Brainstorming is primarily a data-gathering technique; and synectics is similar but more structured and so requires more skill of group members. Consensus thinking is one of the best ways to evaluate data, but it is not always possible to obtain a consensus position. For this reason, we treated various techniques for obtaining a consensus position. The Delphi technique, fishbowling, and didactic interaction can be used to consolidate opinions.

We talked about collective bargaining as it relates to decision making, including their similarities and differences. We presented needs theory as a way to reduce the conflict usually associated with collective bargaining. In the long run, collective bargaining is successful only when both sides implement the principles of rational decision making.

Chapter 6

PERT Analysis

INTRODUCTION

No decision-making text would be complete without a discussion of the fundamentals of the program evaluation and review technique (PERT). Originally developed to manage some rather complex aerospace projects, it is now used to help decision makers manage a wide range of programs from the simple to the complex. The success of PERT is related to the basic logic of the system and to the fact that it is understandable to the manager, who need not get involved with system details. The basic system was created jointly by the Lockheed Aircraft Corporation and the U.S. Navy during development of the submarine-launched Polaris missile system. The Navy believes PERT saved 2 years in this program's development.

USE OF PERT

PERT is used most effectively by working-level managers. It was not intended to be an ivory tower technique that never really gets used by operating personnel. This intention is carried out, in reality, for PERT requires inputs from all areas of a project and thus forces these various factions to interface. As managers from different parts of the organization graphically identify how other groups make decisions that affect the entire program, the result is interdepartmental cooperation in an effort to effectively plan the whole project.

PERT is very useful because it encourages meetings of managers from different departments, and so interface problems can be solved. Thus there is a potential for smoothing working relations among different operating groups, and managers gain respect for the problems of related departments. It is quite common for unsuspected relationships to be discovered. They may emerge when one task cannot be started until a second, apparently unrelated job has been completed. A typical relationship might be the long lead time required to purchase major equipment or long-lead-time material. Because PERT is a dynamic system, it is updated frequently during a project. Thus PERT keeps plans current and identifies constraining relationships that may not have existed when the plan was created.

BASIC SYSTEM

PERT is a graphical technique which uses a chart to describe a project or program. The basic system has only two symbols. A circle is called an *event*, and an arrow is an *activity*. The events are fixed points in time and represent either the start or the completion of an activity. Moreover, an activity is an action which takes time. See Figure 15.

Event 1: Start design   Event 2: Complete design

Activity 1—2: The length of time between the start of the design
              and the completion of the design

Figure 15   Basic event and activity.

When several related activities are placed in serial order on a PERT chart, they form a *path*. A path may consist of many events and activities, or it may be as simple as the path shown in Figure 15. The path allows the user to see in the PERT chart a group of related activities, rather than separate, independent events. The only exception to these rules occurs when an activity requires the expenditure of zero time. For example, suppose an activity is the completion of the design of one item and the start of a second design. This type of activity is referred to as a *dummy* activity, and it requires the expenditure of zero time. Symbolically, a dummy activity is represented by a broken, or dashed, line. See Figure 16.

Figure 16   Dummy activity.

The simplest way to visualize a PERT network is to think of a road map. The path from one point to another on the map may reveal optional routes. These routes may go through different cities and require various amounts of city-to-city travel time. By adding the times between cities and comparing the sums, we can determine the shortest and longest routes. The PERT network does the same thing in that it helps the user discover the best way to complete a project. There is a critical difference between a road map and a PERT network. Only one route is chosen on a road map, and only some cities are visited; in a PERT network, all activities must be completed and all events must occur before the final event can be completed.

A common example of a PERT network is the act of starting the car. Assume that the following events take place before the driver takes a trip in the car.

Event	Activity
1. Start walking to car	1–2 Walk to car
2. Start fishing for car keys	2–3 Fish for keys
3. Start to unlock door	3–4 Unlock door
4. Start to get in car	4–5 Get in car
5. Start to put key in ignition	5–6 Start car
6. Start to roll down window	6–7 Roll down window
7. Start to drive away	

This series of events and activities could be represented by the PERT network shown in Figure 17. Although this figure is complete, it can be

Figure 17   Simple PERT network.

refined. First, locate all activities that can be performed simultaneously. In this example, the driver, while fishing through pockets for keys, could walk to the car. And he or she could start the car and roll down the window at the same time. These are called *parallel* activities. The refined PERT chart is shown in Figure 18.

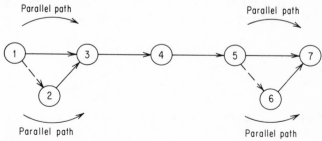

Figure 18   Parallel paths.

Note that Figures 17 and 18 have the same number of activities. Yet, by using parallel paths, the time required to travel the entire path, from start to finish, can be reduced. Also note that the parallel paths do not eliminate any of the activities which must be completed or the events which must take place. Remember, too, that activities can occur simultaneously.

This example is so simple that you now may believe that a PERT diagram is not needed. You are probably right—for the simple diagram presented. But the basic concept just outlined can be used for much more complex programs and projects. No matter how complicated the project, the process starts with two basic steps:

1. List the activities that must be completed to end the program.
2. List the order in which these activities must be conducted. This requires determination of which activities depend on the completion of others.

TIME SCHEDULING

In addition to showing the interaction of events, the PERT diagram is useful in arranging the project's schedule. Time estimates are assigned to every activity and then added to estimate the total time for the project. Figure 19 is a simple PERT chart, similar to Figure 17, with time

Figure 19 Simple PERT network with times indicated.

estimates added for each activity. With this simple diagram, it is easy to see that the total time for the network is 27 seconds.

Figure 20 shows a network similar to Figure 18, except that the total

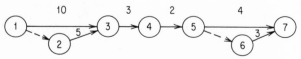

Figure 20 Parallel-path PERT network with times indicated.

time requirements are more complicated. As a result of the parallel paths of Figure 20, the total time requirement is reduced from 27 to 19 seconds. This decrease in the time requirement is a result of the elimination of activities 2–3 and 6–7, which are on parallel and shorter paths.

Clearly, if we wish to complete the project in less time, then we must reduce the time for any one of the activities which are summed to determine the total time needed. Activities that take place on this link in the network are said to be on the network's *critical path*. As we can see from Figure 20, the critical path consists of activities 1–3, 3–4, 4–5, and 5–7. Shortening any one of these activities reduces the total time for the program.

Obviously, a decrease in the time needed to accomplish activity 2–3 or 6–7 will not affect the total time requirement. These activities are said to be on the *slack path*. If Figure 20 represented a process in which we wished to minimize the total time requirement, we would apply additional resources of workers, materials, machines, and so on to items in the critical path. Reducing the time requirement for items in the slack path would have no overall impact. However, when we do apply additional resources, we must be careful not to change the critical path inadvertently. For example, in Figure 20, if activity 5–7 were reduced to 1 or 2 seconds, the critical path would include activity 6–7 in lieu of 5–7. Because the critical path takes the most time to complete, there is only one critical path in a PERT system, except on the rare occasion of two equal-length paths.

The slack time between critical and slack paths is simply the time required for the slack path minus the time needed for the critical path. This information may be quite useful in determining the delay that could be tolerated in activities in the slack path without altering the total time requirement. For example, the slack times in Figure 20 are 5 seconds for activity 2–3 and 1 second for activity 6–7. There is no slack time related to activity 1–3, 3–4, 4–5, or 5–7. This information could be very valuable if we decided, say, to delay resource allocation for a particular activity, knowing that it would or would not affect the total program time. If Figure 20 represented a manufacturing process, it might be logical to redistribute effort from activity 2–3 to activity 1–3. Most likely this would stretch out activity 2–3, but it might also reduce activity 1–3. Since activity 1–3 is on the critical path, probably this action would decrease the time requirement for the project.

TIME ALLOTMENTS

PERT is a method of planning, scheduling, and controlling projects. The planning phase is primarily event-oriented whereas scheduling and controlling are strongly activity-oriented. This means that scheduling and controlling are strongly dependent on time allotments. Therefore, the ability to accurately estimate time requirements for various activities is very important. Only after time estimates are applied to the various activities can the critical path be determined. This step must be taken before rational decisions can be made in relation to controlling the project and scheduling activities for maximum effectiveness.

Time estimates are made most commonly by the people most familiar with the work or by PERT specialists, who come up with estimates from data derived from similar efforts. All estimates must be given in the same units (minutes, hours, days, weeks, and so on), to avoid computational problems and misleading those who review the diagram.

One danger with PERT is that a deadline may be established before the network is completed. When this happens, there is a tendency to force-fit time estimates into the time available. Thus the network may show that all is well when, in reality, the unrealistic time estimates only make it look good. First the network must be defined with realistic time estimates. If the total time required results in bypassing a deadline, then the network should be evaluated to determine which elements of the critical path could have their time requirements reduced.

In all time estimates, there is an element of uncertainty. The PERT system compensates for uncertainty by using three time estimates to calculate a final time estimate—the optimistic, the most likely, and the pessimistic.

The optimistic value, represented by the letter a, is the estimated time to complete an activity when everything goes well. Therefore, estimate a is much shorter than other estimates for the same activity. The most likely time estimate is represented by the letter m. If only one estimate were given for an activity that was neither optimistic or pessimistic, it would be the most likely estimate. The pessimistic time estimate is represented by the letter b. This estimate is large enough to compensate for false starts, poor performance, and other troubles short of fire, flood, and acts of God.

The range between the optimistic and pessimistic estimates is proportional to the uncertainty about the actual time needed to complete the activity. The greater the range, the greater the uncertainty.

This formula computes the expected time (*te*) for an activity by using these three time estimates:

$$te = \frac{a + 4m + b}{6}$$

This formula reveals that the expected time (which is used in the PERT diagram) mostly is affected by the most likely estimate. However, *te* can be greater or less than *m*, depending on whether *a* or *b* deviates more from the most likely value. Obviously, if *a*, *m*, and *b* all have the same value, there is no uncertainty in an activity. For example, take one activity, the curing of a particular chemical mixture, which takes 1 week. If nothing (heat, humidity, chemical composition variance, and so on) can alter this 1-week estimate, then *a*, *m*, *b*, and *te* must be equal. Adding *te*'s for individual activities yields the total time for the project, represented by *Te*. Also *Te* can represent the time accumulated up to a particular event.

DEVELOPMENT OF THE CRITICAL PATH

A key feature of the PERT system is the identification of the critical path of a program. Following this, a number of decisions can be made regarding resource allocation, scheduling, and cost. A system has been devised to identify the critical path. It can be computerized easily, enabling rapid, economical modifications as the program develops. To gain experience with this procedure, let's analyze a simple PERT diagram. Note that the identical procedure would be used for a complex system. For this analysis, we assume that Figure 21 represents the PERT network of a particular program.

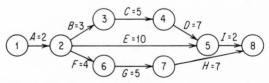

Figure 21 Sample PERT diagram.

To determine the critical path, first, we list the events and the successors for each event. Note that if an event has more than one activity following it, that event is listed more than once. If the expected time is given in the same table, then the table should look like the Table 1.

TABLE 1   Predecessors and Successors

Activity	Predecessor	Successor	te
A	1	2	2
B	2	3	3
C	3	4	5
D	4	5	7
E	2	5	10
F	2	6	4
G	6	7	5
H	7	8	7
I	5	8	2

Second, we compute the earliest start (*ES*) and earliest finish (*EF*) for each activity. For the first activity, the earliest start time is 0. For the first activity, *EF* is simply 0 + *Te*. For subsequent activities, *ES* is exactly the same as *EF* for the preceding activity. For example, *ES* for activity *D* is equal to *EF* for activity *C*. The value of *ES* for activity *I* is whichever is later, *EF* for activity *D* or *E*. Table 2 is the result of these

TABLE 2   Values of the Predecessor,
the Successor, and *ES* and *EF*

Activity	Predecessor	Successor	te	ES	EF
A	1	2	2	0	2
B	2	3	3	2	5
C	3	4	5	5	10
D	4	5	7	10	17
E	2	5	10	2	12
F	2	6	4	2	6
G	6	7	5	6	11
H	7	8	7	11	18
I	5	8	2	17	19

calculations. Now we can find the earliest finish time for the whole program. It is simply the earliest finish time for the last activity to be completed. For our example, activity *H* or activity *I* could be the last activity (depending on the lengths of the preceding paths). Table 2 shows that activity *I* is last because it has the latest *EF* time (19).

Third, we calculate the latest start time *LS* and latest finish time *LF* for each activity that still permit the program to be completed on time. We must start with the activity having the latest *LF* value, activity *I*. For this activity, $EF = LF$. Thus $LS = LF - te = 19 - 2 = 17$. Activity H does not have to be completed before activity I, since both end on event 8, which is the end of the program. Therefore, for activity H, $LF = 19$. For activity H, $LS = LF - te = 19 - 7 = 12$. For other activities, by working backward through the PERT diagram we find that the LS of a given activity equals the LF of the preceding activity. Completing these calculations yields Table 3. Note that the LF of activity A equals

TABLE 3   Values of the Predecessor, the Successor, ES, EF, LS, and LF

Activity	Predecessor	Successor	te	ES	EF	LS	LF
A	1	2	2	0	2	0	2
B	2	3	3	2	5	2	5
C	3	4	5	5	10	5	10
D	4	5	7	10	17	10	17
E	2	5	10	2	12	7	17
F	2	6	4	2	6	3	7
G	6	7	5	6	11	7	12
H	7	8	7	11	18	12	19
I	5	8	2	17	19	17	19

the smallest LS of activities B, E, and F. This is logical since an activity following activity A cannot start prior to the finish of activity A. It follows that the converse is also true.

Activities located on the critical path have tight schedules. As soon as one activity is completed, the next must begin. Activities that are not on the critical path have some acceptable leeway as to when they start, when they finish, and how long they take. Analyzing the data in Table 3 will give us the information needed to make this determination.

To find out whether a given activity has any slack (or how much), we simply review its EF and LF times. If they are equal, then no slack exists and the activity is on the critical path. If they are not equal, then their difference indicates the leeway associated with the given activity. The slack times are not cumulative, because the slack used up by one activity on a slack path is no longer available for future activities on the same path. Table 4 shows the slack times S that result from computing $S = LF - EF$. Table 4 shows zero slack for activities A, B, C, D, and I. This fact identifies both the critical path and the activities that must be accomplished within their estimated times, at penalty of stretching out the total program.

TABLE 4 Slack Times

Activity	LF	EF	S
A	2	2	0
B	5	5	0
C	10	10	0
D	17	17	0
E	17	12	5
F	7	6	1
G	12	11	1
H	19	18	1
I	19	19	0

SCHEDULING

Once we have the PERT diagram, we can utilize this information to establish program schedules. Figure 22 shows a PERT schedule developed from the previous example. A scheduling chart offers a visual rep-

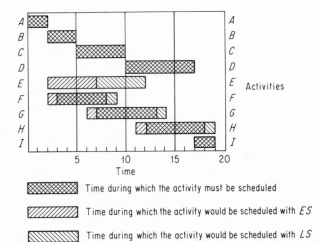

Figure 22   PERT scheduling chart.

resentation of slack. It is easy to visualize, say, that activity E can be started any time between time 2 and time 7, whereas activity C must be started at time 5.

CRITICAL PATH METHOD

The critical path method (CPM) is a management system very similar to PERT. The primary difference is that CPM uses only one estimate to arrive at expected time. Therefore, the time to compensate for uncertainty does not exist. This system is popular in planning programs in which the expected time for an activity can be predicted fairly accurately. This technique is used commonly in the building trades, where severe penalties may be imposed for not meeting scheduled commitments or for projects that have built up a considerable amount of past data on how long it takes to complete portions of the program.

The other variations are superficial. With CPM the circles for the events are eliminated, and the events are called *nodes*. In addition, the arrowheads are eliminated from the activities. With CPM, arrowheads are not attached to the activity lines because the chart always reads from left to right. Often this is done because CPM charts usually are drawn with a time scale. Projecting the length of the activity line on the horizontal scale permits the assignment of a time scale with dates on the horizontal scale. Many users prefer the CPM time-based network because they believe it makes the chart easier to understand and provides a clear visual indication of scheduled event dates. It is easy to make a quick visual check of when activities should be coming to a conclusion. Color coding also assists in tracing program progress and quickly translating it to schedule dates. Those who favor the PERT system believe that CPM is too complicated and is more difficult to update as the program progresses. However, with the development and use of computer-aided graphics, this objection may be overcome.

SUMMARY

The purpose of this chapter was to explain PERT technology. We did not discuss the related topics of resource distribution and leveling, cost analysis, progress reporting, and computer packaging to support the process. Our basic purpose in presenting these data was to provide detail enough for a manager to ascertain whether PERT would be a useful tool for decisions related to the program studied. Few people would argue that the decision maker possessing superior information will make superior decisions. For many programs, a simple bar graph type of schedule is the most appropriate. When a program becomes complex, though, an improved scheduling and tracking system should be considered.

We explained the basic working features of the PERT system. Events were described as points in time and activities as the time-consuming portions of the network. We described the logic of moving from one event to the next and discussed the method of describing parallel paths for simultaneous activities.

Time scheduling and parallel paths were discussed. Then we calculated the expected time for a given activity. The formula modified the most likely time for an activity by potential variations that may be very optimistic or pessimistic.

We used a simplified critical path network as an example and presented a step-by-step procedure to follow. Then we employed a graphical scheduling table to illustrate a bar chart method of displaying critical schedules and slack.

Finally, we talked about using CPM in this type of scheduling system and described differences and similarities of PERT and CPM. Both systems provide an excellent data base for decisions related to project scheduling and progress reviews.

Chapter 7

Force Field
Analysis and QUID

INTRODUCTION TO FORCE FIELD ANALYSIS

Force field analysis is a spinoff of the scientific principle that for every action there is an equal and opposite reaction. Although this idea has been taken for granted in science for many years, it has been ignored in management decision making.

For example, consider a company that is growing. Its growth may be due to a number of factors, such as the superior quality of the product, its lower price, successful marketing, and so forth. But there always exist factors that tend to slow or reverse this growth, such as competition, imports, saturation of the market, decline in top-quality employees, and so on. By using force field analysis, we can identify these "driving forces" and then try to promote those forces assisting us to reach our goal and inhibit or oppose those that are keeping us from moving in the desired direction.

Kurt Levin was a pioneer in the development of the theory of force field analysis.[1] His theory was primarily in the field of human behavior rather than in decision making. But given that human behavior usually is involved in decision making, the two are strongly entwined. Levin believed that a person's behavior in a given environment directly related to the particular person and the environment. Thus, to understand or predict someone's behavior as the result of a management decision, we must know something about the individual and the environment at the time of the decision. Hence, what motivates an individ-

---

[1] K. Levin, *The Conceptual Representation and the Measurement of Psychological Forces,* Durham, N.C., The Duke University Press, 1938.

ual varies with both time and climate in which the person is operating. Levin's field theory was derived from the physicists' concept of the magnetic field; Levin saw human beings as working in a field of various forces and their actions as reactions to these forces.

BASIC CONCEPT

The basic concept associated with a force field analysis is this: in any situation, the forces imposed on the situation are in equilibrium at a given point. This does not mean that forces remain static: rather, at a given instant they are static. Thus the total "driving forces" equal the total "restraining forces." The individual forces may vary in magnitude, but their total does not change.

An example of this balancing of forces could be a manager who stays in the same organization for years. Such things as fair pay, friendliness of coworkers, and interesting work are offset by increased salary opportunities at other companies, travel possibilities in another organization, and so on until one factor changes the balance. This factor could be the removal of an inhibiting force to stay, such as a change in coworkers, or the addition of a driving force, such as the offer of a significantly more challenging position inhouse. Once the balance is disturbed, the situation will find a new balance. For this example, the new balance position might be a new job for the manager.

As a more concrete example, let us review the current level of effectiveness of one manager. Given that we can specify what this effectiveness is, we draw a chart similar to Figure 23. On one side of the chart, we identify the driving forces that tend to push the manager toward higher efficiency; on the other side, we list the factors that tend to push

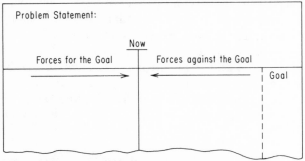

Figure 23   Force field analysis chart.

the manager toward lower effectiveness. The result is shown in Table 5.

Although Table 5 is hypothetical and probably inapplicable or incomplete for any one individual, it does illustrate the type of factors that could be listed for our example. If we want to increase the effectiveness

TABLE 5   Forces Influencing Effectiveness

Current Level of Effectiveness	
Driving Forces to High Effectiveness	Restraining Forces for Low Effectiveness
Supervisory support ———————→	←— Confusing organization
Ambition ———————————→	←— Heavy workloads
Enjoyment of work ———————→	←— Poor MIS*
Desire for status ————————→	←— Heavy turnover
Adequate education ———————→	←— Untrained subordinates
Clear-cut direction ————————→	←— Problems at home
Good health ————————————→	←— Lack of experience
Adequate support staff ————→	←— Poor facilities
	←— Slow supply system
Current financial data available —→	←— Low pay

*MIS stands for management information system.

of the manager, there are two ways to bring about a change. One way is to strengthen or add to the driving forces; the other way is to reduce or eliminate some restraining forces. Of course, any action we might take could precipitate a reaction of a restraining force, actually driving the situation in the opposite direction from the one desired. Let us assume that the company decides to improve the present manager's effectiveness by increasing supervisory support. By itself this could be a desirable move, but it may not be an isolated action. The manager may view the increase in supervisory support as a lack of faith in his or her ability to do the job without close control. This could be a greater factor toward low effectiveness than could possibly have been anticipated originally.

Yet the removal of one restraining force may shift the equilibrium in the desired direction without running the risk of a reaction force. For example, Table 5 reveals that removal of any of the restraining forces would have a highly positive impact with very low risk of a detrimental reaction. Normally it is better to reduce restraining forces than to try to increase driving forces.

FORCE FIELD APPLICATIONS

In the previous example we showed how to use a force field analysis to modify an existing condition. However, use of this system has more far-reaching effects than making changes in an existing status.

Force field analysis can help to unite people from different portions of the organization in order to identify the driving and restraining forces. At times, this interface can be critical in developing a united approach to a chosen course of action. The united approach has a side benefit in that the manager organizing the process can hear both sides of the story. Again, referring to Table 5, we see that one segment of the organization might believe that an enlarged support staff would improve management effectiveness, while another segment might believe that an increased untrained staff would be a detriment.

This technique is applicable in a wide range of business and personal problems. For example, it can be applied to problems involving employee turnover rate, morale level, financial effectiveness, profit, production costs, expenses, customer relations, and so on. As an example, assume that the pending decision involves diversifying or not diversifying the manufacture of a product. First, forces both pro and con could be listed. Many considerations would be financial, but some, both pro and con, would not be financial. For example, both internal organizational modifications and future market prospects must be taken into account. The listing of all the driving and restraining forces could easily uncover an imbalance that could play a significant role in determining the final course of action.

As mentioned earlier, this process can be used in a wide variety of decision-making situations involving personnel decisions. The following is an example of one time when I used the process.

My family always wished we could live in a home on the waterfront. But whenever a home on the waterfront came up for sale that was large enough for my family, it was too expensive. One day we found some waterfront property that consisted of a gigantic house in an excellent location at a price within range. The problem was that the house was very old and badly needed repair. It needed new heating, plumbing, and wiring in addition to storm windows, insulation, and complete redecorating. This sounds like a nice place to avoid. Yet it had an excellent layout, lots of land, and a charm that comes only with turn-of-the-century architecture. The question was, Should we make an offer to buy?

I approached this decision by constructing a force field diagram. Included in my list of approxmiately 20 driving and 20 restraining forces were many financial considerations, such as the inflated price I believed I could get for our existing property and the initial outlay needed to bring the old place to a minimum acceptable standard. With all these considerations written down, I was able to decide two things: that we wanted to buy the property and the maximum price we could pay. This story would have a happy ending if I could report that we bought the property and lived happily ever after. But that did not happen. The owner rejected our offer. However, using force field analysis, I had determined our limit. Nor do I regret that the sale did not materialize, because I learned to identify a fair deal from my perspective, and if we had substantially increased the offer, it would no longer have been a fair deal. Is this situation much different from the procedure a manager would follow to determine the conditions related to potential merger or acquisition that constitute a fair deal?

ANALYSIS PROCEDURE

The previously described procedure has been systematized to provide a common method of use. The following is a straightforward three-step method to go from the description of a problem to a positive course of action.

First, set up a blank piece of paper similar to the one shown in Figure 23. This is logical since the first step in any decision-making situation is to clearly and accurately define the problem. This step should be done in writing, so that it cannot be misinterpreted. The line in the middle of the paper represents the way things are now. The dotted line on the right-hand side of the page represents how you would like things to be.

The problem statement must be all-inclusive; that is, it must completely describe the difference between how things are now and how they ought to be. So the problem statement must cover the people affected, the cause of the problem, the type of problem faced, and goals for improvement or change. If all these are written in the problem statement, it has an excellent chance of being complete and clear.

The goal must be clearly defined. For example, refer to Table 5. The goal could be an increase in effectiveness of managerial staff as measured by an increase of 20 percent of the group's workload with no increase in staff. It is not sufficient to abbreviate the goal to "improve effectiveness." List the driving forces in the direction of the goal on the left-hand side of the paper and the restraining forces on the right-hand side. These restraining forces work against the goal.

In making any decision, you must clearly understand the current situation. The force field offers a clear picture of the forces keeping the situation as it is. It is possible that not all the forces involved actually will be listed, for you may be ignorant of some and consider others insignificant. Since this procedure uses a ranking system, it is important to list as many forces as possible at the start. In the preparation of this list, any of the nonmathematical decision-making techniques described in this text could be used, or your individual judgment could prevail. The choice is yours; however, the advantages of group decision making should be considered.

Second, list these forces in rank order. Take two sheets of paper and list the goal on the top of each sheet. On one, list in rank order the driving forces; on the second, the restraining forces. The first force on the list should be the most important; the second force, the second most important; and so on. Importance is judged by the impact that changing the given force would have on getting closer to the desired goal. A recommended method of creating a ranking is described in Chapter 8, so for the time being you can ignore the mechanics of it.

Another option, which some feel is superior, is to list driving and restraining forces on one sheet in rank order. Although this method might make it easy to list the most important forces first, it ignores the fact that unknown reaction forces may occur if some of the driving forces are strengthened. Hence you should work on the restraining forces before the driving forces. But if you are quite confident that a driving force can be strengthened without a reaction force ensuing, then there seems to be no reason why strengthening these forces would be inappropriate.

In one method commonly used to rank-order the driving and restraining forces, you evaluate each force by how sure you are that it is significant. If some forces require additional data to be understood more clearly, then these data should be gathered. Once you list the forces in relation to how sure you are that they are significant, this list actually represents the rank order of the forces themselves.

Third, you choose a course of action. Select top-priority forces from either the positive or the negative group and describe, in detail, how to implement the plan. This plan should cover what you will do, why you want to do it, and what outcome you hope to achieve. If the course of action involves strengthening driving forces, you must make a serious effort to identify potential reactions and methods of dealing with them. As was mentioned earlier, taking action is not the end, but merely a step in the decision process. Then you must obtain feedback regarding the results of the action taken and possible further action.

QUID

Quantified intrapersonal decision making (QUID) has many similarities to force field analysis, except that an attempt is made to quantify the forces related to intrapersonal decisions, in order to provide guidelines for making good decisions. The system was outlined originally by Jorgensen and Fautsko[2] in 1978, and it has become quite popular in certain decision-making situations. A major difference between the two systems is that force field analysis helps you decide what to do after you consider all forces related to the status quo, whereas QUID is most effective when you must make a go–no go decision. The QUID process is shown in Figure 24.

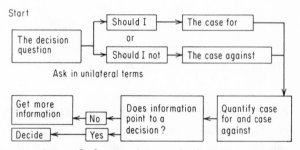

Figure 24 Quantified intrapersonal decision making (QUID) diagram.

QUID follows the same initial procedure as other decision-making processes. Following these five steps will improve your decision-making ability when you use the QUID process:

1. Accurately define the problem and gather all the facts for both sides of the choice. Review these facts carefully and rationally. However, since these facts are related to an interpersonal decision, you should not ignore a "gut" feeling.

[2]J. Jorgensen and T. Fautsko, *QUID—How to Make the Best Decisions of Your Life*, New York, Walker & Co. Publishers, 1978.

2. If you feel driven to make an impulsive decision, spend more time deliberating. While deliberating, rationally list the pros and cons. If, after deliberation, you still decide to follow your original impulse, at least you will have anticipated some possible consequences.

3. Recognize that most decisions can be altered if you are willing to deal with other reactions to your inconsistency.

4. Consider that failure may result if your choice is wrong. This will help you cope better with the potential negative aspects of your decision.

5. When you are stuck and you cannot come to a decision, role-playing the situation with a coworker may help you sort your thoughts and feelings.

THE QUESTION

As noted in Figure 24, the first step in the QUID process is to ask the proper question. This is the yes-or-no question that poses the problem for the decision maker. You should observe four principles when asking this question:

1. The question should be neutral, so put it in value-free form. For example, a "should I or should I not" question does not evaluate the problem, but simply offers two possible options. By its nature, the neutral question forces the decision maker to perform the next logical step—to list the pros and cons of a given action.

2. The question should define alternatives. The "should I" question offers the decision maker options. You must guard against questions that are so value-laden that they leave little choice. There is no way for someone asked the following question to win: "Did you stop beating your wife?"

3. The question should be limited in scope, because the multipronged question is confusing. Avoid questions beginning with "What if" or "How about," because they will lead to a discussion in lieu of a decision. The question must be couched in well-defined terms so that you will recognize a solution when it is proposed.

4. The question should allow for maximum input of ideas. Again, "should I" questions force you to consider all options. When the decision maker begins to think in terms of the case for and the case against, then the decision can encompass the maximum amount of information and provide the means to make a balanced analysis.

QUID ANALYSIS

Once the question to be decided is written down clearly, you should list the case for and the case against taking action. The methods used to list these factors are similar to those employed in force field analysis. However, once the factors are listed, assign points to the factors and average them for each side. Considering the difference between the two averages, you can determine whether the two sides differ enough to make a decision clear. Assign weights to the factors as follows:

Extremely important:	8 points
Very important:	7 points
Important:	6 points
Very significant:	5 points
Significant:	4 points
Of minor significance:	3 points
Worth consideration:	2 points
Worth minor consideration:	1 point

The rule of thumb is as follows: If the difference between the average score for and the average score against is 1 or less, then you should get more information. If the difference is over 1, this suggests a direction for deciding. This guideline does not take the place of the decision maker's judgment; but if the difference of 1 is exceeded, taking action usually is much better than not doing anything.

Also consider the raw score of the total points. If both the raw score and the average score point in the same direction, then you are in a fairly strong position to make a sound decision. However, when the raw score and the average score differ, you should look at how many 6-, 7-, and 8-point factors are going into the raw score. Maybe the accumulation of a few high-point factors is much more important than a larger quantity of minor considerations. Neither the raw score nor the average score is a 100 percent indication, for one large factor may overshadow completely a number of small ones. Clearly an average score can be reduced by adding a factor worth minor consideration to a group of extremely important ones.

To evaluate how many points to assign to a factor, follow these guidelines:

1. *Not a Consideration: 0 Points.* Why should anything be listed that is not a consideration? The reason is usually that someone in the organization suggested it as a factor, but the decision maker believes it to be irrelevant and, therefore, that it should not carry any weight. Listing such a factor simply recognizes that it was not overlooked. But it has no effect on the decision to be made.

2. *Worth Minor Consideration: 1 Point.* Assign a weight of 1 point when a factor is minor and of little consequence to the final decision. You should do this only after you have carefully ascertained that the factor cannot properly be relegated to the "not a consideration" category.

3. *Worth Consideration: 2 Points.* A factor worth consideration definitely will affect the decision.

4. *Of Minor Significance: 3 Points.* This category encompasses items that have some, but not major, significance. You perceive why these factors have varying degrees of importance to some people, but you put them low on your list.

5. *Significant: 4 Points.* This type of factor describes something that plays a serious part in the decision. *Significant* is synonymous with *having meaning*, and any meaningful factor matters; it must be taken into account.

6. *Very Significant: 5 Points.* If *significant* describes something that matters, *very significant* describes something that matters a lot.

7. *Important: 6 Points.* This category includes serious, urgent considerations that inevitably will have far-reaching consequences.

8. *Very Important: 7 Points.* This category takes importance one step further in the direction of urgency.

9. *Extremely Important, or Critical: 8 Points.* This category has the highest weight on the scale. Such a consideration is of the gravest importance; to ignore it would put your final decision in question.

This list attempts to define the gradations of scale to help you assign weights. Your individual subjective values remain a factor in the actual weighting, and undoubtedly they will affect it. However, once you have weighted the factors, the next step in quantifying your decision is to reach a score.

GUIDANCE IN THE QUID PROCESS

The authors of the QUID process believe that if a decision is important enough to be given serious thought, it merits your taking a few minutes to apply the procedures of QUID. Also, to take advantage of QUID, you must use it continuously. The following steps offer guidance in how to make sure, as far as possible, that your final decision is correct.

1. Take some time. Get more information. Look at both sides of the question, and check that you have not omitted anything on either side. Add to the list of considerations as time and situational changes dictate.

2. Rethink the weights assigned to the factors. Compare the weights of various factors. Are factors really assigned a higher number of points as they approach the critical stage?

3. When both the raw score and the average score indicate the same course of action, you are in a strong position to make a good decision. When they differ, you should either gather more information or review the more critical factors. Usually this will point you in the proper direction.

4. The listing and weighting of considerations often can be improved by having more than one person do it. Individuals can do this separately and then compare their scores, or jointly to get one average score.

5. If the decision will affect someone else, then it is a good idea to involve that person in the decision-making process. Add that person's factors to the existing list, or else add the person's score to yours and divide by 2. If a group makes the decision, then most likely the group will help carry it out. However, the decision maker who utilizes a group decision-making process can lose control easily.

6. If a decision still cannot be reached after steps 1 through 5 have been taken, then you should find out whether there is a time limit on the question. If extra time is available, it could be used to gather additional information.

7. Finally, decide. Make the choice based on what you know. Do not stall or leave it to chance. Even if you make an occasional poor decision, you cannot be faulted for using a rational decision-making process.

ASSISTING DECISION MAKERS

At times you will be requested to help someone else make a decision. This is an extremely difficult position to be placed in. If your advice is good, you may be considered an unnecessary step; but if it is poor, prepare to take full credit for your advice. The following checklist can help you decide whether to get involved at all. Although not all 10 items must be checked, the more items that are checked, the more likely you are to be of assistance.

1. The request for help is sincere, not simply a courtesy.
2. The problem is real, not one made up to get attention.

3. The person presenting the problem actually has the problem.

4. The person knows enough about the problem to provide a data base.

5. You can relate to the problem and empathize with the person having the problem.

6. You can devote enough time to help solve the problem.

7. You have some practical experience in rational decision making.

8. You have a good grasp of how rational decision making works.

9. You truly believe that you can help the person asking for assistance.

10. You wish to become involved.

SUMMARY

In this chapter we presented the fundamental concept that any situation is controlled by a number of forces acting on it. The forces push or pull in opposite directions, and by identifying them it is possible to control the direction they will take. In a yes-or-no decision, the proper direction can be determined by quantifying the relevant factors.

The processes described in this chapter can be modified significantly without destroying the underlying principle, provided three steps are followed:

1. Forces must be identified.

2. The forces must be studied in relation to their importance.

3. The decision should be made based on the information available and the desired outcome.

Chapter **8**

Moody's Precedence Charts

INTRODUCTION

I consider the procedure outlined in this chapter to be a significant new contribution to management decision making. As a result, this chapter may be longer than some others, for there is no other source of literature to supplement this material.

The precedence chart was developed as a simple method to assist the decision maker who is considering a number of alternative courses of action. Normally, as the number of options grows, so does the difficulty of selecting the best one. If the options overlap in both favorable and unfavorable aspects, then the final decision becomes even more difficult to make. We present a simple mathematical method of listing items by their relative importance (precedence) without bias and without the necessity of comparing more than two items at a given time. This systematic approach to rank-ordering options from least to most favorable can be applied to a number of decision-making situations.

The basis for using the precedence chart is the assumption that the simplest and most accurate choice results from direct comparison of two alternatives. This procedure is not a substitute for sound judgment, which must be used in comparing the two options. However, by considering only two possibilities at a time, we can use the precedence chart as a decision-making tool.

We provide four variations of the precedence chart with examples of their use. The mathematics is very simple, but it is always possible to make an error. Therefore, for each variation we make an overall mathematical check that determines if the total number of comparisons is correct. The four variations are identified as follows:

Simple precedence chart
Multiple-input weighted precedence chart

Combined precedence chart
Extension of precedence chart use

Note that all the examples in this chapter are for illustration only, and only minor consideration is given to the factors listed.

SIMPLE PRECEDENCE CHART

The simplest, and perhaps the most widely applicable, use of the precedence chart is to help a manager list alternatives by order of importance. First, we establish a basis for evaluating the factors that will comprise the list. For example, referring to Table 5 (in Chapter 7), assume that we wish to list, in order of priority, the factors that are a detrimental influence on a particular manager's effectiveness. The purpose is to identify the factor with greatest influence, so that we can make a primary effort to reduce that influence. So we write a question to be used as a basis for the list. For this example, we use the following question: Which factor reduces management effectiveness most?

Second, we list possible items to consider. We can do this by brainstorming, executive decision, group meeting, or any other method. The total number of items in the list is not important. But the longer the list, the more time is required to work out the mathematics of the solution. So we list similar items together and discard any obviously irrelevant suggestions. For example, suppose brainstorming is used to obtain replies to our question. One suggestion is, "The manager's office is too small," and a second, "The manager lacks adequate file space." These could be combined in a general category entitled "poor facilities." However, if a suggestion is made that the manager's effectiveness was reduced because the place of employment was not located in Bermuda, we could eliminate this as an irrelevant factor, because it is a *given* factor, which cannot be changed. For this example, we list in priority order the factors cited as restraining forces in Table 5. To use them with the precedence chart, we number each factor as shown in Table 6.

How easy it would be if we only had two forces to prioritize. We could simply make a choice and work on the factor selected. Unfortunately, this example is not so simple. So the third step is to make a 10 × 10 matrix for 10 factors (or a 19 × 19 matrix for 19 items, and so on). Then we list the factor numbers on the left and top of the chart. Next we trace out all squares, diagonally from the upper-left-hand corner down to the lower-right-hand corner, and write the question above the chart. We

TABLE 6 List of Factors

Factor	Restraining Force
1	Confusing organization
2	Heavy workload
3	Poor MIS
4	Heavy turnover
5	Untrained subordinates
6	Home problems
7	Lack of experience
8	Poor facilities
9	Slow supply system
10	Low pay

also list the factors on the left-hand side. For this example, the resulting chart looks like Figure 25.

Once a chart has been drawn, the fourth step is to individually compare factor 1 with the other nine factors. We begin by comparing factors 1 and 2. We ask, Which factor reduced management effectiveness

Which factor reduces management effectiveness the most ?

Row factors		Column 1 2 3 4 5 6 7 8 9 10
Confusing organization	1	
Heavy workload	2	
Poor MIS	3	
Heavy turnover	4	
Untrained subordinates	5	
Home problems	6	
Lack of experience	7	
Poor facilities	8	
Slow supply system	9	
Low pay	10	

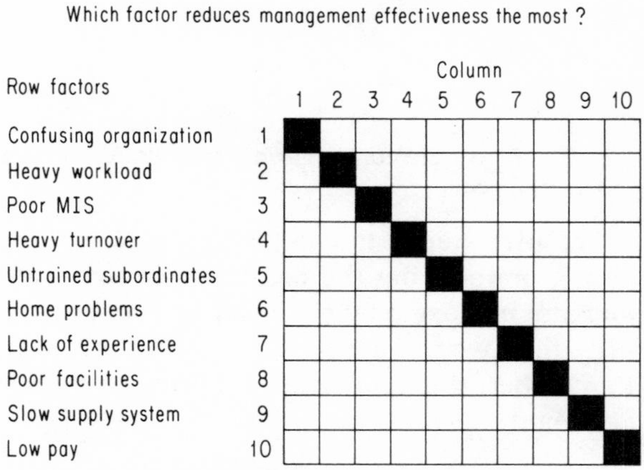

Figure 25 Blank precedence chart.

the most—the confusing organization, or the heavy workload? For example, say that we decide that the heavy workload has a greater influence than a confusing organization. Figure 26 indicates that if we have to choose between factor 1 and factor 2, then factor 2 (heavy workload) takes precedence. For this comparison a 0 is placed in row 1, column 2, and a 1 goes in row 2, column 1.

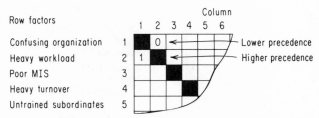

Figure 26 Precedence chart with a single comparison.

To save time and avoid confusion, we could omit labeling the rows. The chart still indicates that the heavy workload has a greater influence than a confusing organization. See Figure 27.

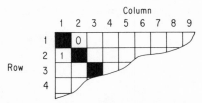

Figure 27 Single-comparison precedence chart with labels omitted.

The fifth step is to compare items 1 and 3. If we decide that eliminating or reducing the confusion in the organizational structure will increase management effectiveness more than making improvements in MIS, then we put a 1 in row 1, column 3, and a 0 in row 3, column 1. Remember, this represents a direct comparison of items 1 and 3 only. See Figure 28.

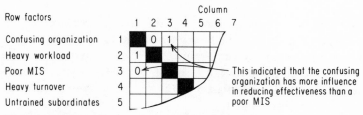

Figure 28 Precedence chart with two comparisons.

After we compare factor 1 with each other factor, we get a chart that looks like Figure 29. Note that diagonally opposite blocks contain a 1 and a 0. Diagonally opposite blocks never have two 0s or two 1s.

The sixth step is to compare factor 2 with the remaining eight factors. For the first comparison, assume that heavy workload has a greater

Which factor reduces management effectiveness the most ?

Row factors		Column									
		1	2	3	4	5	6	7	8	9	10
Confusing organization	1		0	1	0	0	0	0	1	1	1
Heavy workload	2	1									
Poor MIS	3	0									
Heavy turnover	4	1									
Untrained subordinates	5	1									
Home problems	6	1									
Lack of experience	7	1									
Poor facilities	8	0									
Slow supply system	9	0									
Low pay	10	0									

Figure 29 Precedence chart with one factor evaluated.

influence on reducing management effectiveness than a poor MIS. In this case, a 1 is placed in row 2, column 3, and a 0 is placed in row 3, column 2. This indicates that if we had to choose between items 2 and 3 only, item 2 would take precedence (see Figure 30).

We compare factor 2 with all the other factors, one by one, until all the boxes in row 2 and column 2 are filled. Then we compare factor 3

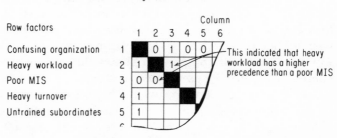

Which factor reduces management effectiveness the most ?

Row factors		Column					
		1	2	3	4	5	6
Confusing organization	1		0	1	0	0	
Heavy workload	2	1		1			
Poor MIS	3	0	0				
Heavy turnover	4	1					
Untrained subordinates	5	1					

This indicated that heavy workload has a higher precedence than a poor MIS

Figure 30 Precedence chart with a second factor comparison.

with each of the remaining seven factors. This completes row 3 and column 3. We continue this process until we have compared each factor individually with every other factor and placed a 1 in the row with highest precedence.

Once the chart is completed, we add the number of 1s in each row and place their sum at the right of the chart (see Figure 31). The factor

Which factor reduces management effectiveness the most ?

Row factors		1	2	3	4	5	6	7	8	9	10	Total
Confusing organization	1	■	0	1	0	0	0	0	1	1	1	4+
Heavy workload	2	1	■	1	1	1	0	1	1	1	1	8
Poor MIS	3	0	0	■	0	0	0	1	1	1	1	4
Heavy turnover	4	1	0	1	■	0	1	1	1	1	1	7
Untrained subordinates	5	1	0	1	1	■	1	1	0	1	1	7+
Home problems	6	1	1	1	0	0	■	1	0	1	1	6
Lack of experience	7	1	0	0	0	0	0	■	0	1	1	3
Poor facilities	8	0	0	0	0	1	1	1	■	1	1	5
Slow supply system	9	0	0	0	0	0	0	0	0	■	1	1
Low pay	10	0	0	0	0	0	0	0	0	0	■	0

45

Figure 31 Completed simple precedence chart.

having the highest number in the Total column has the highest precedence. The factor with the next highest number in the Total column has the next highest precedence. We continue until all items are listed in precedence order, from most to least important.

On two occasions the total on the right (for two rows) is the same. We know that the higher the number, the higher the precedence in our final listing. So to determine the relative importance of two tied items, we look at their individual comparisons and put a plus sign next to the one with higher preference. In this example rows 1 and 3 had totals of 4. But the individual comparison shows that when factors 3 and 1 are compared, factor 1 has greater significance than factor 3. Therefore, we put a plus sign next to row 1. The original comparison is reflected by the 1 in column 3, row 1, and the 0 in column 1, row 3. The same holds with items 4 and 5. Column 5, row 4, contains a 0 whereas column 4, row 5, contains a 1. So we put a plus sign to the right of row 5.

If a three-way (or more) tie occurs, a subprecedence chart may be required, but this is rarely necessary. As an example, suppose we removed a number of items from the total list in order to compare them with one another. If we compared factors 1, 2, and 3 individually, say, we would get a chart like Figure 32. Note that the 1s and 0s are in the

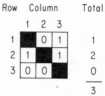

Figure 32 Subprecedence chart.

same location as on the original, larger chart in Figure 31. We find that factor 2 has top priority with factor 1 second, and factor 3 last. If only these three factors are considered, factor 2 is the most significant.

We establish the simple precedence order by listing the factors in order by which factor had the highest number in the Total column. See Table 7.

TABLE 7 List of Factors in Precedence Order

Precedence No.	Total Points	Factor No.	Primary Factors that Reduce Effectiveness
1	8	2	Heavy workload
2	7+	5	Untrained subordinates
3	7	4	Heavy turnover
4	6	6	Home problems
5	5	8	Poor facilities
6	4+	1	Confusing organization
7	4	3	Poor MIS
8	3	7	Lack of experience
9	1	9	Slow supply system
10	0	10	Low pay

It is possible to create a precedence chart by exactly the opposite procedure—assigning a 1 and a 0 to the individual comparisons. Thus the factor with the lowest number would have the highest precedence. Possibly the factor with total points equal to 1 would have first precedence, the factor with total points of 2 would have second precedence, and so on. This method of analysis is valid, but we do not recommend it, because the possibility of confusion outweighs the slim probability of having the factors end up in their exact precedence order.

We offer a second example to emphasize the importance of determining and stating the question, at the top of the chart, prior to completing it. Let us modify the previous question thus: Which factor will be the easiest to modify in order to increase management effectiveness? A procedure identical to that of the previous example is followed, and the results are shown in Figure 33. The precedence order has changed significantly, as shown in Table 8.

Which factor will be the easiest to modify to increase management effectiveness?

Row factors		Column 1	2	3	4	5	6	7	8	9	10	Total
Confusing organization	1	■	0	1	1	1	1	0	0	1	0	5
Heavy workload	2	1	■	1	1	1	1	0	0	1	0	6
Poor MIS	3	0	0	■	0	0	0	0	0	0	0	0
Heavy turnover	4	0	0	1	■	0	1	0	0	0	0	2
Untrained subordinates	5	0	0	1	1	■	1	0	0	1	0	4
Home problems	6	0	0	1	0	0	■	0	0	0	0	1
Lack of experience	7	1	1	1	1	1	1	■	0	1	0	7
Poor facilities	8	1	1	1	1	1	1	1	■	1	1	8
Slow supply system	9	0	0	1	1	0	1	0	0	■	0	3
Low pay	10	1	1	1	1	1	1	1	1	1	■	9

45

Figure 33 Simple precedence chart for a revised question.

TABLE 8 List of Factors for Revised Question

Precedence No.	Total Points	Factor No.	Easiest Factor to Modify
1	9	10	Low pay
2	8	8	Poor facilities
3	7	7	Lack of experience
4	6	2	Heavy workload
5	5	1	Confusing organization
6	4	5	Untrained subordinates
7	3	9	Slow supply system
8	2	4	Heavy turnover
9	1	6	Home problems
10	0	3	Poor MIS

It is interesting how a factor that had the lowest priority can jump to the highest priority when a different basis for comparison is used. In this illustration, the movement of the factor "low pay" from position 10 to position 1 may indicate that increasing a manager's salary is the easiest thing to do but results in only a short-term increase in effectiveness, whereas relieving the heavy workload results in some long-term increase in management effectiveness.

MATHEMATICAL CHECK FOR SIMPLE PRECEDENCE CHART

Without a complete review of each factor, it is impossible to ensure that a 1 and a 0 were not inadvertently placed in the wrong blocks. Also, without a complete check of all addition it is impossible to determine whether one addition error canceled another. However, we can check quickly whether the total number of comparisons made matches the proper number for the variables considered. We use this formula:

$$T = \frac{n(n-1)}{2}$$

where T = total number of comparisons and n = number of items considered.

For both previous examples, the total number of comparisons is

$$T = \frac{10(10-1)}{2} = \frac{10(9)}{2} = 45$$

Note that 45 is the total number of comparisons for these examples. This formula works regardless of the number of items. For example, consider the subprecedence chart in Figure 32, in which only three factors are considered:

$$T = \frac{n(n-1)}{2} = \frac{3(3-1)}{2} = \frac{3(2)}{2} = 3$$

Referring to Figure 32, we see that the total number of comparisons is 3.

MULTIPLE-INPUT WEIGHTED PRECEDENCE CHART

The previous examples illustrated the basic concept of the precedence chart; however, not all comparisons are that simple. Assume that an organization is required to list all its projects by precedence and, as a cost reduction process, the three considered the least likely to be successful are canceled. Assume further that the organization is divided into four departments and each must list its three low projects. Once this is done, a meeting is held of all four department heads and their supervisor to select three projects from the entire organization to be canceled. In a large organization with many complex projects, it may be quite difficult for a single top manager to listen to each department head and choose 3 of the 12 candidates to be canceled. When a democratic method of decision making is employed, it may be difficult for each department head to defend his or her projects and simultaneously make an unbiased list of potential candidates. Let's say that each of the five people involved in the decision has an equal voice in the selection. For example,

Department 1 lists projects *A*, *B*, and *C*.
Department 2 lists projects *D*, *E*, and *F*.
Department 3 lists projects *G*, *H*, and *I*.
Department 4 lists projects *J*, *K*, and *L*.

First, we decide what we wish to compare and state the question exactly. Second, we draw a 12 × 12 matrix (since there are 12 projects) and then ask each department head to explain the merits and shortcomings of the three projects she or he listed. Following this explanation, we begin the comparisons, one by one. Say that three people believe project *A* should be dropped instead of project *B* and two people believe the opposite. If a simple majority were to rule, we would fill in the chart as in the previous examples, with a 1 in row 1, column 2, and a 0 in row 2, column 1. However, the closeness of the decision would be reflected on a multiple-input precedence chart (Figure 34) by recording a 3 in row 1, column 2, and a 2 in row 2, column 1.

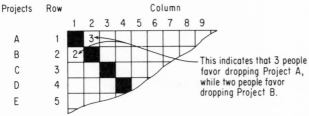

Figure 34 Multiple-input weighted precedence chart—first comparison.

We follow this procedure until all the spaces are filled as before except that each pair of squares totals 5. The final chart looks like Figure 35. Table 9 lists the projects in priority order.

In a listing with many items, projects having the same number of points are less likely, because the point span is considerably wider. The

Which project has the least possibility of being successful ?

Projects	Row	Column												Total
		1	2	3	4	5	6	7	8	9	10	11	12	
A	1	■	3	4	5	3	2	4	1	3	4	5	3	37
B	2	2	■	3	4	3	3	4	2	3	4	5	1	34
C	3	1	2	■	2	3	2	4	2	4	5	5	2	32
D	4	0	1	3	■	3	1	3	2	5	3	4	4	29
E	5	2	2	2	2	■	0	2	3	3	3	4	3	26
F	6	3	2	3	4	5	■	4	4	2	4	5	3	39
G	7	1	1	1	2	3	1	■	2	3	3	4	3	24
H	8	4	3	3	3	2	1	3	■	2	3	5	4	33
I	9	2	2	1	0	2	3	2	3	■	3	3	2	23
J	10	1	1	0	2	2	1	2	2	2	■	4	4	21
K	11	0	0	0	1	1	0	1	0	2	1	■	1	7
L	12	2	4	3	1	2	2	2	1	3	1	4	■	25

330

Figure 35 A completed multiple-input weighted precedence chart.

method also may reflect grouping of projects. In our example, precedence numbers 1 through 5 appear in one group, numbers 6 through 11 appear in another group, and apparently precedence number 12 (project K) should never have been included since it has a high possibility of being successful. By this process project F is identified as hav-

TABLE 9   Projects Listed by Precedence Order

Precedence No.	Total Points	Project	Precedence No.	Total Points	Project
1	39	F	7	26	E
2	37	A	8	25	L
3	34	B	9	24	G
4	33	H	10	23	I
5	32	C	11	21	J
6	29	D	12	7	K

ing the least possibility of being successful. We could make another comparison at a future date (after F had been eliminated) to determine whether project A still would be identified as the next most likely to be dropped.

Another variation of the multiple-input precedence chart is the weighted precedence chart. As in the previous example, we assume that each department head has a 1-point vote and the top manager a 3-point vote. Therefore, if the department heads are split 2 to 2 over whether project A or B has the least possibility of success, the top manager's preference to list project A must have a considerably greater weight. This is illustrated in Figure 36. The remainder of the process is identi-

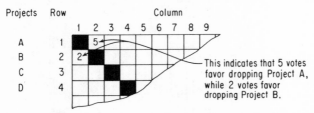

Figure 36 Weighted precedence chart with first comparison.

cal. It is easy to see how varying the weights of individuals can greatly affect the final outcome. The entire process can be simplified by using a majority rule with weighted votes and a system of 0 or 1 point on the chart (as in Figure 31).

Still another variation of this procedure may be used by a single individual or group. Two items are assigned weights indicating how desirable one item is with respect to the other. For example, if a total point count of 6 is used, the weights might be as follows:

A	B	
0	6	B has much greater precedence
1	5	B has greater precedence
2	4	B has slightly greater precedence
3	3	Equal precedence
4	2	A has slightly greater precedence
5	1	A has greater precedence
6	0	A has much greater precedence

As an example, we assume that five individuals in a branch are being considered for promotion to a branch head position. Each has strengths and weaknesses and varies in personality, ability, and education. Only one person can be offered the position. However, we want to establish a precedence order of potential branch heads, because the person selected might refuse the position. For this example, the basic question is, Who should be offered the branch head position. Potential candidates are Smith, Jones, White, Black, and Brown.

The weights for comparing these five individuals are as follows:

3–3   Evenly distributed capabilities
2–4   One person is superior in any one category of personality, overall ability, or education
1–5   One person is superior in two categories of personality, overall ability, or education
0–6   One person is superior in all three categories of personality, overall ability, and education

Smith is the best educated of the group. However, this may not be sufficient to make Smith the first choice when all the factors are considered. For example, if we compare Smith with Jones and Smith has a superior education, Jones has a superior personality, and they are equal in overall ability, then their weighted comparison is 3–3. If Jones has a superior personality and overall ability, then their weighted comparison is 2–4 in favor of Jones. A completed chart looks like Figure 37.

From Figure 37 it is clear that Brown should be first choice. What if Brown refuses the job? Is the choice then White? Not necessarily! We determine who should be offered the position next by crossing Brown

Who should be offered the branch head position ?

Candidates	Row	Column					Total
		1	2	3	4	5	
Smith	1	■	2	3	3	2	1 0
Jones	2	4	■	1	2	4	1 1
White	3	3	5	■	2	2	1 2
Black	4	3	4	4	■	0	1 1
Brown	5	4	2	4	6	■	1 6
							6 0

Figure 37 Weighted precedence chart for five candidates.

from the list and calculating new totals. We must do this because we are working with a priority of the remaining four candidates, not five. If we cross out column 5 and row 5, we get the chart shown in Figure 38.

Figure 38 reveals that the actual top candidate is Black. The purpose of this illustration is only to show that although all alternatives must be

Who should be offered the branch head position ?

Candidates	Row	Column					Total	New total
		1	2	3	4	5		
Smith	1		2	3	3	2	10	8
Jones	2	4		1	2	4	11	7
White	3	3	5		2	2	12	10
Black	4	3	4	4		0	11	11
Brown	5	4	2	4	6		16	
							60	36

Figure 38   Weighted precedence chart for four candidates.

considered, only the potential candidates should be used for the final analysis. What if Black refuses the job? We cross Black from our chart, as in Figure 39.

Now White becomes the number 1 choice. If White refuses the position, then Smith and Jones are the only candidates left. From Figure 38

Who should be offered the branch head position ?

Candidates	Row	Column					Total	New total	New total
		1	2	3	4	5			
Smith	1		2	3	3	2	10	8	5
Jones	2	4		1	2	4	11	7	5
White	3	3	5		2	2	12	10	8
Black	4	3	4	4		0	11	11	
Brown	5	4	2	4	6		16		
							60	36	18

Figure 39   Weighted precedence chart for three candidates.

they appear tied. However, when we remove the points for White, Smith ends up in direct comparison to Jones. Jones, superior in two of the three qualifications for the position, is selected. We assume that all qualifications have equal weight. If they do not, things become a bit more complex. However, we discuss this later in this chapter.

MATHEMATICAL CHECK OF MULTIPLE-INPUT WEIGHTED PRECEDENCE CHART

The mathematical check of the multiple-input weighted precedence chart is very similar to that of the simple precedence chart, except the total number of points used for each comparison must be considered:

$$T = \frac{n(n-1)}{2}(p)$$

where T = total number of comparisons
n = number of items considered
p = number of points assigned per comparison

For the previous illustrations, the total number of comparisons is as follows:

For Figure 35, a 12-project list by four department heads and one top manager (total = 5 points per set of blocks):

$$T = \frac{12(12-1)}{2}(5) = \frac{12(11)}{2}(5) = \frac{132}{2}(5) = 330$$

For Figure 36, a 12-project list by four department heads and one top manager with a weighted preference of 3 times any of the department heads (total = 7 points per set of blocks):

$$T = \frac{12(12-1)}{2}(7) = \frac{12(11)}{2}(7) = \frac{132}{2}(7) = 462$$

For Figure 37, a weighted system for listing five candidates for a position with a 0 to 6 weight balance (total = 6 points per set of blocks):

$$T = \frac{5(5-1)}{2}(6) = \frac{5(4)}{2}(6) = 60$$

For Figure 38, a weighted system for listing four candidates for a position with a 0 to 6 weight balance (total = 6 points per set of blocks):

$$T = \frac{4(4-1)}{2}(6) = \frac{4(3)}{2}(6) = 36$$

For Figure 39, a weighted system for listing three candidates for a position with a 0 to 6 weight balance (total = 6 points per set of blocks):

$$T = \frac{3(3-1)}{2}(6) = \frac{3(2)}{2}(6) = 18$$

COMBINED PRECEDENCE CHART

So far we have been very careful to take into account only one factor when utilizing a precedence chart. However, very often more than one factor must be considered and more than one question asked in determining the final precedence order.

As an example, let's return to the original problem of how to list the factors that reduce management effectiveness. Assume that we are equally concerned with which factors are the most influential and which are easiest to modify to increase effectiveness. The most straightforward method to establish a combined precedence list is to complete preliminary precedence charts, as in Figures 31 and 33. Next we mathematically combine (or add) their results, as in Table 10.

If two items combine to the same number of points, put an asterisk next to the one with the higher individual point count in either list, to

TABLE 10 Preliminary Combined Precedence List

Figure 31		Figure 33		Combined Totals	
Factor No.	Points	Factor No.	Points	Factor No.	Points
1	4+	1	5	1	9+
2	8	2	6	2	14
3	4	3	0	3	4*
4	7	4	2	4	9
5	7+	5	4	5	11+
6	6	6	1	6	7
7	3	7	7	7	10
8	5	8	8	8	13
9	1	9	3	9	4
10	0	10	9	10	9*

indicate its higher precedence. If they are truly tied, note that on the final list. For our example, the final listing is shown in Table 11.

It is interesting that a combined list yields a precedence different from that in either Table 7 or Table 8 when both questions are taken into consideration. It is also easy to visualize more than two charts being prepared and then combined in a similar manner.

TABLE 11 Combined Precedence List

Precedence No.	Total Points	Factor No.	Factor
1	14	2	Heavy workload
2	13	8	Poor facilities
3	11+	5	Untrained subordinates
4	10	7	Lack of experience
5	9+	1	Confusing organization
6	9*	10	Low pay
7	9	4	Heavy turnover
8	7	6	Home problems
9	4*	3	Poor MIS
10	4	9	Slow supply system

Precedence charts also can be combined when a weighted factor is used in the evaluation. For example, assume that in our previous example it is twice as important to identify the easiest factors to modify as the most influential. The tabulations are shown in Table 12. The final list is shown in Table 13.

TABLE 12 Preliminary List of Weighted Combined Precedence

Figure 31				Figure 33				Combined Points	
Factor No.	Points	Weight	Subtotal Points	Factor No.	Points	Weight	Subtotal Points	Factor No.	Points
1	4+	1	4+	1	5	2	10	1	14+
2	8	1	8	2	6	2	12	2	20
3	4	1	4	3	0	2	0	3	4
4	7	1	7	4	2	2	4	4	11
5	7+	1	7+	5	4	2	8	5	15+
6	6	1	6	6	1	2	2	6	8
7	3	1	3	7	7	2	14	7	17
8	5	1	5	8	8	2	16	8	21
9	1	1	1	9	3	2	6	9	7
10	0	1	0	10	9	2	18	10	18

TABLE 13   Weighted Combined Precedence List

Precedence No.	Total Points	Factor No.	Factor
1	21	8	Poor facilities
2	20	2	Heavy workload
3	18	10	Low pay
4	17	7	Lack of experience
5	15+	5	Untrained subordinates
6	14+	1	Confusing organization
7	11	4	Heavy turnover
8	8	6	Home problems
9	7	9	Slow supply system
10	4	3	Poor MIS

Again, the precedence order has changed. This points out quite dramatically how the entire process is only a tool; management's judgment on weights to be placed on each variable is of major consequence.

EXTENDING THE USE OF THE PRECEDENCE CHART

The previous methods of establishing precedence are useful if the list is to help determine which action to take first, in which order to attack a problem, which item should be financed, and so forth. But what if all the items listed influence a decision and the list is used to determine which item should have greater weight in the final evaluation of a multiple proposal?

For example, assume our goal is to design a revolutionary automobile, and we have three design proposals A, B, and C to choose from. Using one of the precedence chart procedures, we determine the following order of desirable features for this automobile:

1. Low initial cost
2. High resale value
3. Economy of operation
4. Good warranty
5. Durability
6. Safety
7. Ease of operation
8. Style
9. Comfort
10. Extras

It is easy to see not only that this order yields a precedence of desirable features, but also that we would be foolhardy to ignore comfort completely for the sake of reducing the initial cost. To resolve this dilemma, first we determine how much more important feature 1 is than feature 10. Is it 10 times as important or only twice as important? Once this decision is made, the rest of the process follows a system.

Say we wish to evaluate three designs, and we feel feature 1 is twice as important as feature 10. We could use weights of 2 and 1, but then fractional weights would be assigned to features 1 through 10. It simplifies the mathematics to assign a weight of 9 to feature 10 and a weight of 18 to feature 1. The proportion of weights between features 1 and 10 remains unchanged. For the time being, you have to take this on faith, because the method of deriving and using these ratios is explained later in the chapter.

Once each of the three proposals has a list of feature weights, each proposal must be evaluated mathematically with acceptability criteria. For this example, assume we use the following criteria:

Criteria Weight	Provided by Design Proposal
3	High acceptability
2	Medium acceptability
1	Low acceptability
0	Nonexistent

Comparing the three proposed automobile designs yields Tables 14, 15, and 16.

TABLE 14 Evaluation of Proposal A with 2:1 Feature Weight

Precedence No. of Features	Feature Weight	Criteria Weight	Total Weight
1	18	3	54
2	17	2	34
3	16	0	0
4	15	1	15
5	14	3	42
6	13	2	26
7	12	2	24
8	11	2	22
9	10	3	30
10	9	2	18
		Total =	265

**TABLE 15   Evaluation of Proposal *B* with 2:1
Feature Weight**

Precedence No. of Features	Feature Weight	Criteria Weight	Total Weight
1	18	3	54
2	17	2	34
3	16	3	48
4	15	2	30
5	14	3	42
6	13	2	26
7	12	2	24
8	11	2	22
9	10	0	0
10	9	1	9
		Total =	289

**TABLE 16   Evaluation of Proposal *C* with 2:1
Feature Weight**

Precedence No. of Features	Feature Weight	Criteria Weight	Total Weight
1	18	1	18
2	17	2	34
3	16	0	0
4	15	2	30
5	14	2	28
6	13	3	39
7	12	2	24
8	11	3	33
9	10	2	30
10	9	3	27
		Total =	263

For purposes of illustration, we use the same number of high, medium, low, and nonexistent acceptability points (criteria weights) for each proposal. This is not necessary, but it shows how the location of high and low weights affects the total weight. For our example, proposal *B* is selected for further development because it has the most points.

Suppose in our previous example we had determined that feature 1 was 10 times more significant than feature 10. Then we could assign a weight of 10 to feature 1 and 1 to feature 10. Assigning the same criteria weights and evaluating exactly as before, we find Tables 17 through 19.

Regardless of the weight factor, the priority order of the three proposals is always *B*, *A*, and *C*. This is true under the artificial condition in which each proposal uses equal quantities of criteria weights (0s, 1s, 2s, and 3s). However, in actual use, the number of criteria weights is not identical for each proposal, and this could cause a change in the final priority order.

Also note that in these illustrations we used straight-line weights when evaluating features 1 to 10. However, this is not necessary, and any relationship (exponential, stepped, group, and so on) between the top- and lower-priority features can be established as long as it is con-

TABLE 17   Evaluation of Proposal *A* with 10:1 Feature Weight

Precedence No. of Features	Feature Weight	Criteria Weight	Total Weight
1	10	3	30
2	9	2	18
3	3	0	0
4	7	1	7
5	6	3	18
6	5	2	10
7	4	2	8
8	3	2	6
9	2	3	6
10	1	2	2
		Total =	105

TABLE 18   Evaluation of Proposal *B* with 10:1 Feature Weight

Precedence No. of Features	Feature Weight	Criteria Weight	Total Weight
1	10	3	30
2	9	2	18
3	8	3	24
4	7	2	14
5	6	3	18
6	5	2	10
7	4	2	8
8	3	2	6
9	2	0	2
10	1	1	1
		Total =	131

TABLE 19   Evaluation of Proposal _C_ with 10:1 Feature Weight

Precedence No. of Features	Feature Weight	Criteria Weight	Total Weight
1	10	1	10
2	9	2	18
3	8	0	0
4	7	2	14
5	6	2	12
6	5	3	15
7	4	2	8
8	3	3	9
9	2	2	4
10	1	3	3
		Total =	93

sistent among proposals. Also note that this method of evaluation is not limited to 10 factors. Any number of factors can be used and the weights varied to suit the application. For example, if 23 items are to be ranked and the most important is 3 times as important as the least important, then item 1 could have a weighted value of 33 and item 23 a weighted value of 11, because $33 \div 11 = 3$.

A numerical system could be used as a method of establishing an acceptability level. For example, if a set of criteria is established by publishing company executives for a certain type of book, first they determine the weight value for each of the criteria they believe to be important. Their second step is to apply the weighted value analysis to books that they consider successes and those they consider failures. If their evaluation is correct, then two groups of point counts are established. Now, when a new text is submitted for review prior to possible publication, it could be evaluated realistically as to its probability of success.

MATHEMATICAL DETERMINATION OF WEIGHT FACTORS

It is desirable to use whole numbers for the weight determination to simplify the mathematics and reduce the possibility of mathematical errors. With the following formulas we calculate the weight factors to be used:

$$\text{HWF} = \frac{n(r) - r}{c}$$

$$LWF = \frac{HWF}{r}$$

$$i = \frac{HWF - LWF}{n - 1}$$

where HWF = highest weight factor
LWF = lowest weight factor
i = interval between factors
n = number of factors
r = relative importance of top factor to lowest factor
c = common denominator for all weights

At times, the common denominator c cannot be identified before HWF and LWF are found. For example, if HWF = 90 and LWF = 9, then c would equal 9. Thus HWF and LWF could be reduced to 10 and 1 respectively.

For 10 items, with the most important item twice as important as the least important (n = 10, r = 2, and c = 1) we have the following (see Tables 14, 15, and 16):

$$HWF = \frac{10(2) - 2}{1} = 18$$

$$LWF = \frac{18}{2} = 9$$

$$i = \frac{18 - 9}{10 - 1} = 1$$

For 10 items, with the most important item 10 times as important as the least important (n = 10, r = 10, and c = 1):

$$HWF = \frac{10(10) - 10}{1} = 90$$

$$LWF = \frac{90}{10} = 9$$

Obviously, if HWF = 90 and LWF = 9, then a common denominator of c = 9 can be used to reduce HWF and LWF to their lowest whole numbers. Therefore, the calculation must be redone with n = 10, r = 10, and c = 9 (see Tables 17, 18, and 19):

$$HWF = \frac{10(10) - 10}{9} = 10$$

$$\text{LWF} = \frac{10}{10} = 1$$

$$i = \frac{10 - 1}{10 - 1} = 1$$

For 23 items, with the most important 3 times more important than the least important ($n = 23$, $r = 3$, and $c = 1$), we get the following:

$$\text{HWF} = \frac{23(3) - 3}{1} = 66$$

$$\text{LWF} = \frac{66}{3} = 22$$

With HWF = 66 and LWF = 22, a common denominator of $c = 2$ will reduce HWF and LWF as follows:

$$\text{HWF} = \frac{23(3) - 3}{2} = 33$$

$$\text{LWF} = \frac{33}{3} = 11$$

$$i = \frac{33 - 11}{23 - 1} = 1$$

SUMMARY

These procedures illustrate only some of the numerous variations and uses of the precedence chart principle. There are too many other examples to enumerate, but here is a partial list of possible uses:

1. Rate personnel for a job
2. Evaluate functions of a position
3. Do performance evaluations
4. Evaluate capital expenditures
5. Determine sequence of events on a schedule
6. Organize daily work
7. Organize change in company structure
8. Prioritize jobs
9. Delegate tasks
10. Rate prospective employees

This method of determining priorities may be considered by some to be more complex than a simple selection. However, when the number of factors to be considered is large, it is impossible for one person to keep everything straight unless a systematic approach is taken. This point can be illustrated easily when a group attempts to make a joint decision without a systematic approach. The pros and cons may be repeated many times without a decision on priority ever being reached unless a long time is expended or someone with authority takes the lead of the conference. In a classroom in which several groups have been asked to list items by priority, I have explained the process to my group, followed the procedure, and achieved more accurate results in less time than the competitive groups. Not only does the procedure enable its user to arrive at a better decision, but also the people involved in the decision process realize that an unbiased systematic approach was taken and so are much more likely to agree with and back up the conclusions reached.

Note the following points:

1. A precedence chart does not take the place of good, solid decision making, but it is a valuable tool.
2. The simple precedence chart is easy to remember and execute and thus should have the widest applications.
3. The methodology of the precedence chart is such that a computer program can be created to state the comparisons to be made, store in memory the choices made, and print out the final precedence listing. This program eliminates the possibility of mathematical error and might reduce the management time required to use the precedence chart procedure.

Chapter **9**

Decision Trees

UNCERTAINTY

In reaching a decision, not only must the problem itself be analyzed and clearly defined, but also the people and costs must be taken into account along with the method to be used. Many times a number of courses of action are possible, each with an uncertainty associated with its result. When reviewing the available courses of action, the decision maker always has the option of delaying a decision until further data can be gathered which might provide insight into the results of the various choices. However, delaying a decision usually has an associated cost. This cost may be in terms of time, work force, money, or numerous other things (which are not always identified or even expected). Eventually the decision maker must make judgments about the uncertainties and choose a course of action. The course of action selected reflects the decision maker's preference for the consequences implied by that action. But there is always some uncertainty. Sometimes it can be identified. When this can be done, the decision maker can take into consideration both the uncertainties and the potential courses of action and perform an analysis to determine the best course of action.

EXAMPLE OF A DECISION TREE

The best way to describe the operation and use of a decision tree is with the use of an example. To set up an example or an actual case, a number of factors must be specified, such as possible courses of action, which are available as soon as the problem is described. We should include the option of gaining additional information and assessing its impact on the decision process.

Let us assume that a company has an option to import and sell a product made in a foreign country. The product will be new in the United States, and its market potential is not known with certainty.

However, we can anticipate that known products, similar to this one, are unsuccessful, nominally successful, or very successful. Figure 40 shows a preliminary decision tree for these data.

Note that Figure 40 has two symbols, a square and a circle. The square represents a decision point for the decision maker; the circle

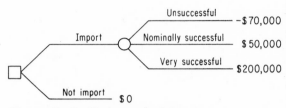

Figure 40   Preliminary decision tree.

represents a point of chance where something will happen, but the exact outcome cannot be predicted. There are three possible outcomes if we decide to import the product: a potential loss of $70,000, a gain of $50,000, or a big gain of $200,000. We also have the option of not importing the product at all, in which case money is neither gained nor lost.

However, assume there is still another option—to analyze the product's market in an attempt to predict its potential success. In fact, two market analysis schemes are possible, with each having a different cost and a different accuracy regarding its success record. Thus we expand our decision tree in Figure 41 to reflect two more branches than are shown in Figure 40.

Figure 41 shows all the courses of action as well as the costs associated with market testing—$10,000 for test A and $20,000 for test B. Furthermore, Figure 41 shows the probabilities of unsuccessful, nominally successful, and very successful product distribution. Also shown is a probable distribution of market test results. As expected, the market test has a possibility of poor, average, and good results, with the same probability as the total population. Now, many textbooks explain that the probability of obtaining various results by market testing need not be the same as the potential success for the product itself. Although this is true, in our case any variation could be attributed only to errors introduced by the testing method, assuming that there is no error in test sample selection.

Market test *A* can predict any of three results: poor, average, or good. However, once the market test has indicated that the market is good, for example, the actual probability of the venture being very successful is much greater than that for a random sample with no data base. This is true when the test predicts poor sales, since the chances of the ven-

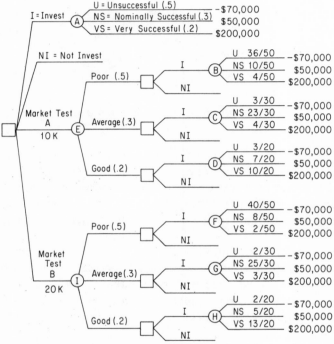

Figure 41 Full decision tree.

ture being unsuccessful are increased. This is only logical, because it would be a waste of money to spend $10,000 on a market test and be in no better position after the market test. The numbers under the final right-hand branches indicate the probability of the end result, which is dependent on the test result.

The $20,000 market test *B* is a better predictive tool than market test *A*. It should be, because it costs more. For example, if test *A* indicates a poor market, then there is a 35:50 chance of it actually being a poor market. If test *B* predicts a poor market, then there is a 40:50 chance of it being a poor market.

By now you should be thinking that this is all well and good, but where did all these numbers come from? If so, you have grasped what could be considered the weakest part of the analysis. These figures may not be available to an individual who works independently or for a small company. If this is the case, it would be better to make the original choice by hunch, or conjecture, because the analysis will not be time-effective. However, a big company or a company that has access to data (perhaps from a consultant company) can develop these figures. In fact, if a company intends to remain in the same speculative field, their past efforts should be quantified so the data can provide guidance for future decisions. For our example it is not too difficult to quantify the three most probable outcomes of an important venture. Although figures could be found anywhere between the maximum loss and maximum profit, it is not uncommon to be able to identify nominal maximum, minimum, and average figures. It is also possible to find the frequency with which each state occurs. As for the probabilities of a market analysis being able to predict product success, that is the purpose of a market analysis. It should be anticipated that a more in-depth (and more expensive) market analysis should be more accurate in its prediction.

All the probabilities associated with each point of chance must add to unity—no more and no less. This is true regardless of the location of the point in the tree. For example, the poor-results branch has a probability of .5. The chance point, located farther down the invest branch, is based on portions of 50 (.5 $\times$ 100) simply for mathematical ease.

The toughest part of any decision tree is setting it up. Most managers assign this task to a subordinate. However, they should be familiar enough with the process to be able to question the source of the data on the diagram. For our example, the following mathematics applies. For clarity, each chance point is labeled with a letter so that we can follow the diagram and compare it with the calculations.

For no market analysis (point A):

$$
\begin{array}{rl}
(.50)(-70) = -35 & \text{(a 50\% chance of losing \$70,000)} \\
(.30)(50) = 15 & \text{(a 30\% chance of making \$50,000)} \\
(.20)(200) = \underline{40} & \text{(a \underline{20\%} chance of making \$200,000)} \\
20 & 100\%
\end{array}
$$

On the average, an import scheme such as this yields a profit of $20,000, without any market analysis.

The calculations for market test A are as follows (the rationale for the remainder of the points is the same as for point A):

Point B:

$$\frac{36}{50}(-70) = -50.4$$
$$\frac{10}{50}(50) = 10.0$$
$$\frac{4}{50}(200) = \underline{16.0}$$
$$-24.4$$

Point C:

$$\frac{3}{30}(-70) = -7.0$$
$$\frac{23}{30}(50) = 38.3$$
$$\frac{4}{30}(200) = \underline{26.7}$$
$$58.0$$

Point D:

$$\frac{3}{20}(-70) = -10.5$$
$$\frac{7}{20}(50) = 17.5$$
$$\frac{10}{20}(200) = \underline{100.0}$$
$$+107.0$$

These calculations show that if we decide to conduct market test A, we will gather additional data regarding the potential profit or loss of the venture. How much is this worth—*before* the test is given? We can find out by taking the answers at points B, C, and D and calculating the combined market-test value:

Point E:

$$.5(-24.4) = -12.2$$
$$.3(58.0) = +17.4$$
$$.2(107.0) = \underline{+21.4}$$
$$+26.6$$

Thus the value of going into the venture and conducting market test A is \$26,700. However, market test A costs \$10,000. So the cost of the test must be subtracted from the average profit of \$26,700, or \$26,700 − \$10,000 = \$16,700. On a straight mathematical average, it is better to go into the venture without a market test, since the average of \$20,000 is greater than \$16,700.

What about market test B? Is it worthwhile? To find out, we perform a similar analysis:

Point *F*:

$$^{40}\!/_{50}(-70) = -56$$
$$^{5}\!/_{50}(50) = 8$$
$$^{2}\!/_{50}(200) = \underline{8}$$
$$-40$$

Point *G*:

$$^{2}\!/_{30}(-70) = -4.7$$
$$^{25}\!/_{30}(50) = 41.7$$
$$^{3}\!/_{30}(200) = \underline{20.0}$$
$$57.0$$

Point *H*:

$$^{2}\!/_{20}(-70) = -7.0$$
$$^{5}\!/_{20}(50) = 12.5$$
$$^{13}\!/_{20}(200) = \underline{130.0}$$
$$135.5$$

Point *I*:

$$.5(-40) = -20.0$$
$$.3(57) = 17.1$$
$$.2(135.5) = \underline{27.1}$$
$$24.2$$

However, market test *B* costs $20,000, so we subtract $20,000 from the average profit of $24,200, winding up with a net profit of $4200.

Therefore, before taking any steps at all, we can see that, on the average, going directly into the venture with no market analysis results in a $20,000 gain. With market test *A* there is a $16,700 gain, and with market test *B* a $4200 gain. Again, these are all based on averages.

What should we do? Although the mathematics is cut and dry, the decision is not. A large investor probably can afford to play the averages and invest with no market analysis. However, what if you are a small investor and the loss of $70,000 will wipe you out? Then the picture changes. You may be willing to sell out your option immediately for $20,000 and eliminate all risk. A big investor who can afford the risk may be willing to buy at a maximum of $20,000. However, will he? Most likely not, since the big investor has access to the same analytical capabilities as you. The big investor will try to buy for less than $20,000. This is the point at which negotiation will take place, since you may be willing to settle for less than $20,000 on a sure thing. Thus the rich get richer and the poor settle!

There are other options, though. What if you can afford a market analysis but not the loss of $70,000? Looking at the potential payoffs for market tests *A* and *B*, you immediately discard *B*, even though it may be more accurate, because its total net worth is less than that of market test *A*.

So you gamble with $10,000 and hope for the best. If the test shows a poor market, then you have moved down the decision tree to the point related to poor results of market test *A*. With an average loss of $24,400 predicted (point *B*), should you invest? Should you not invest and absorb the $10,000 expense of the market test? Should you sell your rights to the product? If the potential buyer knows about the poor pre-diction of the market test, most likely you will have great difficulty in trying to sell your rights. If not, should you inform the buyer? Since this book is about decision making, not morality, we do not try to answer. However, if you do hide pertinent facts related to a sale, you can expect the deceit to be revealed and the company to be labeled as one to avoid.

What if market test A shows average results? If you invest, you can expect an average $58,000 profit (point C). If you subtract the $10,000 invested in the market test, you still have an average profit of $48,000. This would certainly put you in a better position to sell your rights for a greater amount, just as if good results had been indicated. The $107,000 average profit at point D minus $10,000 for the test surely would put you in a desirable position.

What is the answer? According to the analysis, you should go into the venture with no test market. However, this decision can be modified, depending on your ability to absorb potential losses and your personal preference for or against risk.

STEPS IN A DECISION TREE

The previous example is only one possible use of the decision tree pro-cess. It can be employed in many cases in which payoffs are known or can be estimated and the probability of various results can be calcu-lated. Even if this information is not available, the decision tree experi-ment can be beneficial. The benefit may not come directly from the calculation, but rather from the construction of the decision tree dia-gram. Setting up the diagram makes the decision maker aware of all available options and possible consequences. The diagram itself may force the decision maker to consider options which she or he would not otherwise consider. In addition, the decision maker may recognize that some consequences should be avoided, regardless of the probability of their occurrence.

In any case, there are four essential steps in a decision tree analysis:

1. Lay out the diagram of the decision problem in the form of a decision tree. Show the chronological interaction of alternate courses of action, and distinguish between chance and decision points. It is a good idea to label all the decision and chance points in order to properly label and check the calculations.

2. Assign the payoffs to the tips of the trees. This is best done by using statistics from similar past efforts. If this type of data cannot be obtained, it can be estimated. However, the more the estimation, the greater the risk of basing a decision on data that may be misleading.

3. Assign probabilities to each of the chance branches. It is best to base these data on statistics from past events. However, it is possible for both the probabilities and the potential payoffs to take maximum and minimum values, and so you perform the analysis twice. The danger, though, is that payoffs and probabilities may overlap, making the final data inconclusive.

4. Select the best strategy by doing the necessary calculations. Averaging the data provides an indication of what branch to follow if the individual's preference for risk avoidance is not taken into account. If risk avoidance is considered, the decision maker must choose how much to sacrifice in potential earnings for the sake of eliminating risk.

PERFECT INFORMATION

How much is perfect information worth? To find out, let's return to our previous example. We do make one modification: we eliminate the branch related to market test *B*, since the value of perfect information would be the same for both market tests *A* and *B*. Also, we eliminate the branches indicating that the decision can be made to not invest if perfect information reveals that the investment is a sure winner. Also we get rid of the invest branch if the market test indicates a sure loser. See Figure 42.

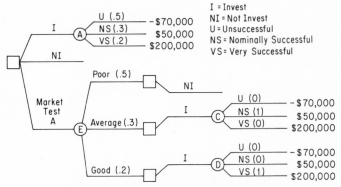

Figure 42 Decision tree with perfect information.

As before, the value of the project without the market test is $20,000:
Point A:

$$.5(-70) = -35$$
$$.3(50) = 15$$
$$.2(200) = \underline{40}$$
$$20$$

However, the value at point E has changed considerably. The reason is that the perfect market test eliminates the possibility of pursuing the branch resulting in a sure loss.
Point E:

$$.3(50) = 15$$
$$.2(200) = \underline{40} \quad \text{with perfect information}$$
$$55$$

Classical decision making theory tells us that the value of perfect information is the difference between the average project value and the value once success has been ensured: $55,000 - $20,000 = $35,000. Note that this figure is the same as that calculated by multiplying the .5 probability of loss by 70, the maximum loss.

The preceding analysis is classical. We believe it is also in error. To illustrate the error of placing too much stock in calculations, let's take another example and vary the figures. For this case we assume that an investment has a 50:50 chance of success and we can either win or lose $100,000, depending on the outcome. This is similar to flipping a coin for $100,000. We also assume that a method exists to predict the outcome of the flip with 100 percent reliability. How much is it worth to be able to make this prediction? By the classical method of analysis, Figure 43 defines the decision tree. The values at the two points are, respectively:
Point A:

$$.5(-100) = -50$$
$$.5(100) = \underline{50}$$
$$0$$

Point B:

$$.5(100) = 50$$

Therefore, we theorize that it is worth $50,000 to accurately predict the outcome of the coin toss. Does this sound logical? Is it worth $50,000 to predict the outcome of the coin toss? If we find out we are going to lose, then we do not toss the coin at all and end up losing $50,000 for the test. If we find out we are going to win, then we reduce our winnings by the cost of the information gained, or $100,000 − $50,000 = $50,000. If we repeated this experiment many times, by the law of aver-

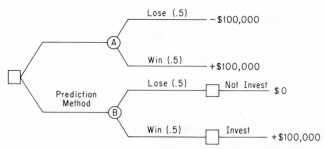

Figure 43   Perfect information for a win-lose situation.

ages we would end up even. However, if we do obtain information for less than $50,000, we continue to gain. Hence, $50,000 is the maximum we will pay for the information. This does not mean what we actually pay for the information, because a $50,000 payment takes away all our potential profit. Remember that these examples use averages and statistics. But since seldom does the exact same problem occur in a business environment more than once, it is best to tend to conservatism unless one has a gambling instinct and can afford the potential losses.

ANALYSIS DISAGREEMENTS

As with many theoretical analysis techniques, there is not universal agreement on the proper process to follow. The primary disagreement concerns the method of analyzing the combined value of the branches once one branch has been determined a loser. For example, the combined value of market tests *A* and *B* could be modified considerably if the branch containing the poor results were eliminated. The logic in arguing for eliminating the unprofitable branch is that no rational person would ever pursue a direction most likely to result in a loss. The argument for keeping the loss in the computation is that prior to the test we do not know whether it will indicate poor, average, or good results. In the previous computation we kept the loss in the computation. Now we repeat the calculations, eliminating the poor branch:

Point E:

$$.3(58.0) = 17.4$$
$$.2(107.0) = \underline{21.4}$$
$$38.8$$

Point I:

$$.3(57) = 17.1$$
$$.2(135.5) = \underline{27.1}$$
$$44.2$$

Clearly, the rationale has changed considerably. In fact, these figures predict a completely different direction to pursue. Now the value of point E is still reduced by the $10,000 cost of market test A, but $38,800 − $10,000 = $28,800. The value of market test B is $44,200 − $20,000 = $24,200. Thus conducting either test is better than going into the venture with no information. Market test A is superior to B, since its net value is higher, $28,800 versus $24,200.

Which method of analysis is correct? We believe the first is right, but this is not universally accepted. The actual decision most likely will be made as a result of the decision maker's preference, financial situation, and personal degree of risk avoidance. For example, one manager is content to make the calculation at point A, determine that the probabilities indicate that the venture is a good one, and avoid any market analysis effort, for he sees market analysis as cutting into his final profit, regardless of by how much. Another manager may make the same calculation and recognize that on the average she will do all right. At the same time, she recognizes there is a 50 percent chance of losing $70,000. This fact alone may drive her to insist on a market analysis, reducing the probability of such a loss. A third manager may perform the same analysis and decide to sell immediately, thus eliminating all risk and opting for a possibly smaller, but sure profit.

SUMMARY

In this chapter we explained the decision tree concept of mathematically reducing the risk of uncertainty. The concept is rather simple, yet the greatest value of the process can be realized by assigning potential profit, loss, cost, and probability figures to the branches. This assignment is the most difficult part of the process, because the data may not be readily accessible.

As in all management decisions, there is always the option of doing nothing or selling out a potential course of action. These options cannot be ignored, since they are always present and on most occasions indicate the path of minimum risk. However, the usual rule is small risk, small profit; large risk, large profit. Unfortunately, a similar rule is small risk, small loss; large risk, large loss.

The most critical portion of decision tree analysis is the first step, the proper construction of the decision tree itself. If branches are ignored or potential outcomes overlooked, the analysis may completely miss a key point. Once the tree is set up, numbers must be assigned to various branches to enable a mathematical analysis to be made.

The value of perfect information is more of an exercise in logic than a true consideration for a manager. However, it does point out that additional information has a price tag attached to it, and the manager who continues to study a problem to death is certain to invest more than the correct solution can repay.

The disagreement about including branches with negative potential in a combined effort is overshadowed by the individual decision maker. Each decision maker's attitude toward risk is unique to the individual, and if figures alone were used to make decisions, some of the innovative adventures we are familiar with never would have occurred.

10

The Value of Information

INTRODUCTION

There can be little doubt that the value of information is directly proportional to the expense of making a poor decision or the reward associated with a good decision. If the expense involved in making a decision is high or the reward associated with it is low, then expending a great amount of time, effort, or money to gather facts cannot be justified. But if the consequences of making an improper decision are serious or the rewards of a good decision extensive, then a considerable expense associated with gathering information about the problem certainly can be justified.

As an example, suppose you are to select an individual to fill a vacancy within the organization. If the position carries considerable authority in either policy or the expenditure of significant capital investments, then you should take great care in the selection process. You should consult personal interviews, reference investigations, educational background studies, and a review of each applicant's record before you choose someone to fill the position. This type of investigation entails considerable expenditure of time and effort; however, a wrong person in a key position could be disastrous to the organization's future.

Now suppose you are to select an individual to fill a lower-level position in the organization. Perhaps you are interested only in determining whether the individuals have the necessary skills to perform the basic job functions. For example, what are the speed and accuracy requirements for a typist? What are the visual requirements for an inspector? What are the educational requirements for a junior engineer? If you make a mistake in filling one of these positions, you can rectify it by either retraining or removing the individual from the position with a minimal impact on the overall organization. This concept is shown in Figure 44.

ANALYSIS OF EXTREMES

One method of determining how much information needs to be gathered before a decision can be reached is the analysis of extremes. By this method the extremes for each alternative are examined and the

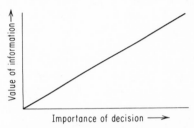

Figure 44 Importance of decision versus value of information.

potential impact of things going very well or very poorly is determined. If even the extreme consequences are rather insignificant, clearly it is illogical to spend a great deal of effort gathering information. If the consequences could have a great impact on the future, then data gathering becomes vital.

The following examples illustrate this concept. They also illustrate that the impact on the extremes of each alternative should not be assessed without all relevant factors being taken into account.

The first decision involves the selection of a typist for a typing pool from several qualified applicants. A casual review of the position could easily lead you to conclude that little information gathering is appropriate. You may believe that the worst consequence of selecting someone who takes no pride in the work is an imperfect letter, and no one will really care. This could be true. But what if the position requires the typing of either computer cards or involved accounting data? Errors in these two cases could cause considerable time to be expended in finding out why a computer program failed to operate properly or accounting data did not balance. To make things even more complex, what if the typist's work is displayed on a screen for easy correction or is reviewed by a senior person? Does this factor make the task of gathering background information less important in choosing an applicant? Quite possibly.

The second decision involves the selection of a junior engineer. Does making a decision about this position require the gathering of more information than for the typist position? It depends. If the individual chosen has lots of unchecked authority, then more information about the candidate may be needed. For example, the junior engineer whose duties include the selection of strength members for a product must be extremely competent. But it is not so important to obtain data about the background of a junior engineer whose calculations are reviewed by senior staff as a safety check. This example is not meant to imply that only the negative aspects of a decision should be considered. If the junior engineer turns out to be such a superstar that he or she can develop a new method of analyzing strength members, manufacturing costs could be reduced significantly. In this case, choosing the best person becomes more important, and so more background information should be gathered about the applicants before the decision is made.

These examples show that the relationship between the value of information and the importance of a decision is not as straightforward as in Figure 44. A secondary influence also must be considered—the extent of controls imposed versus the freedom of action once the decision has been made. Figure 45 illustrates this principle.

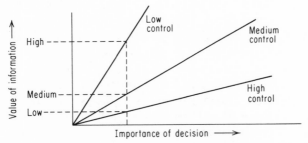

Figure 45   Importance of decision versus value of information in relation to the extent of control.

Figure 45 shows that for any given decision, the value of information is inversely related to the control over the consequences of the decision. In the previous examples, the value of the work performed by the typist or junior engineer is inversely related to the controls imposed after the decision is reached. Is their work reviewed? How closely? What is the consequence of either superior or inferior work? Once these questions have been answered, it is possible to determine the value of gathering additional information before the decision is reached. As expected, with high control there is little need to gather a great deal of information. Conversely, if low control follows a decision, it becomes important to gather more information before the decision is made.

VALUE OF TIME

Often we hear the statement, "Time is money." Well, there is a good reason why this phrase is so common. It is true in most cases. Not only is there a direct cost related to the effects of gathering relevant facts, but also there is a cost, frequently overlooked by the decision maker, called the *opportunity cost*.

The opportunity cost can be identified numerically, as demonstrated later in this chapter; however, the quantification of such a loss is subject to a number of assumptions. This may be good for textbook learning and the practice of developing a logical line of thought, but often it is not applicable in the real world. The opportunity cost, which is usually much more real and much more difficult to get a handle on than the direct cost, is the nonquantifiable cost.

For purposes of illustration, we differentiate between quantifiable and nonquantifiable opportunity costs thus:

1. Quantifiable opportunity costs can be identified easily as losses, as the result of hard data. As an example, your company imports foreign-made goods, and you estimate the demand for a particular item to be 10,000 units. You cannot reorder these items. You can make a profit of $2 for each item you distribute. After advertising the item, you receive orders for 15,000 units. You completely drain your inventory of these items and must refuse orders for 5000 units, because you simply cannot meet the demand. The quantifiable opportunity cost in this situation is the 5000 units you cannot deliver times the profit lost by not filling all the orders. In this example, the opportunity cost is 5000 units times $2 per unit, or $10,000.

2. A nonquantifiable opportunity cost cannot be identified as a specific loss, as the result of hard data. As an example, given the same conditions as in item 1, the initial decision is made that the item would have only a minimal demand, and so none are imported. Since you import no items, you do not advertise the item, and so you receive no orders.

As you know from the previous example, if you had advertised the item, you would have received orders for 15,000 units. But you cannot know this if you never advertise. You can estimate how many orders you might have received, but it is no more than a guess. If you had been convinced of the number of orders that would have been received, you would have imported that quantity and made your profit.

3. Another form of nonquantifiable opportunity cost is incurred in the data gathering designed to help make a decision. In the previous example, the nonquantifiable opportunity cost could be the cost of conducting a marketing survey. Although the actual cost of the survey can be determined, the cost related to the time needed to conduct the survey cannot be quantified. For example, assume our marketing survey indicates that this import venture will be profitable. We select a quantity to import and swing into our advertising campaign. For this example, it is immaterial whether the resulting orders exceed or are less than the quantity imported. The point is, there is no way to know whether there would have been more or fewer orders had the delay associated with the marketing survey not occurred. Did this delay in advertising the product permit a competitor to move in? Did the customers' taste change? If either case actually occurred, then clearly the time factor impacted the profit or loss realized. We had the opportunity to act rapidly, but we failed to do so, and an opportunity cost probably will be incurred. But we cannot quantify this cost.

STRATEGY

Up to this point, we provided very little concrete data about how much to expend in time or money in order to gather information to make a decision. There is a good reason: there is no magic formula that provides this information. In fact, each decision is unique and must be treated accordingly. However, some guidance is possible.

You should develop a winning strategy for decision making. This means that given similar conditions, your decisions should follow a pattern. Decisions vary in subject matter, timing, associated circumstances, personal involvement, and so on. The trick is to develop a winning strategy and avoid a losing one.

How can you do this? The answer is really quite simple. Observe others! Note how they make their decisions and the results. People learn nothing by having their mouths open, but gain all their knowledge and abilities by keeping their eyes and ears open. Here are some examples.

A young engineer joins a firm and has high hopes of being a success. He should pay particular attention to other engineers in the company who have been both successful and not successful. He should note which group makes quick decisions, what data each group gathers prior to making a decision, the person sought out by the successful individual for data or advice. How much detailed data is gathered, and how do the groups interface with other parts of the organization? A careful evaluation of these factors and others peculiar to the organization reveals two strategies in relation to the group's actions. Then the engineer must establish a strategy that correlates with those of people using a proven, successful decision-making technique.

As a second example, suppose you have a particular skill and want to go into business. The problem is that you do not want to incur the risk and expense of trial-and-error decision making regarding marketing, finance, legal decisions, buy-or-rent decisions, personnel practices, and so on. The best way to become familiar with the decision-making strategy of a field is to join a firm having a good record in a similar field. It may be a sound investment in time (even if the salary is less than desired) to observe firsthand how the decision-making strategy of the company pays off. If you disagree with a course of action taken by the company, it might be particularly interesting for you to evaluate the results of the chosen course of action. With hindsight, you can judge the results of the decision and compare them with what you project would have been the results of your choice of action. Be very careful not to fool yourself by looking at your potential results through rose-colored glasses.

When choosing a strategy to follow, be sure you identify all ingredients, including those that are not obvious. The primary ingredient is time. A strategy may be quite applicable if aimed at short-term results and quite inappropriate if aimed at long-term results. One simple example is your decision to scrape or not scrape your house prior to painting. The decision may relate more to how long you plan to live in the house than to which method produces the better paint job. This type of thinking is seen many times in the military. A military man has a limited time at any one duty station. He must make a recognizable contribution in that time. This pressure may influence his ability to make unbiased tradeoffs between long-term programs and those with a more rapid payoff. Someone who is unaware of such outside influences could mistake the strategy for solving a particular problem as being applicable to only that problem, when actually the strategy relates more to other influences that impact the problem-solving technique.

MATHEMATICAL SOLUTION

In many cases a mathematical solution to a problem is not applicable. The reason is not that the mathematics is incorrect, but that the data needed for the equations is lacking.

If data is available, it would be foolish not to use it as a guide. As an example, recall the import problem involving opportunity costs. If the import business has been in existence for a number of years, there should be a record of what moves and what does not. If this data is current and orders are categorized by the type of product imported, it could be quite useful. Assume that by reviewing the data we determine that this type of product is demanded in accordance with Table 20. (A frequency of .05 indicates that 0 units are ordered 5 percent of the time,

TABLE 20 Order Frequency for One Type of Import

Quantity Demanded	Order Frequency
0	.05
5,000	.15
10,000	.30
15,000	.30
20,000	.15
25,000+	.05

a frequency of .15 indicates that 5000 units are ordered 15 percent of the time, and so on.)

Next, after determining the order frequency from history, we construct a conditional profit and loss chart. For this example assume that we suffer a loss of $1 for each unit that we stock and is not ordered. For each unit we order and distribute, we make a profit of $2. See Table 21.

TABLE 21 Conditional Profit and Loss Chart (Dollars)

Possible Demand	Possible Supply					
	0	5,000	10,000	15,000	20,000	25,000
0	0	−5,000	−10,000	−15,000	−20,000	−25,000
5,000	0	10,000	5,000	0	−5,000	−10,000
10,000	0	10,000	20,000	15,000	0	5,000
15,000	0	10,000	20,000	30,000	25,000	10,000
20,000	0	10,000	20,000	30,000	40,000	35,000
25,000	0	10,000	20,000	30,000	40,000	50,000

The logic behind Table 21 is as follows. If we supply 0 units, we have no costs; nor can we fill any orders. Therefore, the profit or loss is zero. If we supply 5000, 10,000, 15,000, 20,000, or 25,000 units and the demand is zero, we suffer a loss of $1 for each unit we ordered—$5000 loss for an overstock of 5000 units, a $10,000 loss for an overstock of 10,000 units, and so on.

If we supply 5000 units and 5000 are demanded, we make $2 per unit, or $10,000. If we supply 5000 units and demand increases, we still make $10,000, since we cannot fill the extra orders. If we supply 10,000 units and only 5000 are ordered, we make $10,000 for the 5000 units sold but lose $1 each for the 5000-unit overstock. This yields a net gain of $5000.

If we order 10,000 units and sell them all, we make $20,000; however, any orders over and above what we can supply give us no more than the $20,000. In reality, there may be an opportunity cost and a hidden loss related to this condition, for we may lose the customer's good will if we are out of stock frequently. Customers may be obliged to seek another supplier. But for now we assume that the low stock level incurs no tangible cost. If we supply 15,000 units and only 5000 are ordered, we lose $10,000 for the overstock and gain $10,000 for the units that were demanded. These figures balance, so the net result is zero. If we supply 15,000 units and 10,000 are demanded, we gain $20,000 from the units demanded and lose $5000 from the overstock. The net gain is $15,000. Other figures in the profit and loss chart are calculated in similar fashion, until all the blocks are filled in.

Note that Table 21 assumes that both supply and demand functions are in increments of 5000 units. In real life, these functions could take any value in between these 5000-unit increments. However, for mathematical simplicity both supply and demand figures are clustered around these numbers.

Via Table 20, we know the frequency with which we can expect each demand function to occur. We can multiply each row by the frequency we established for the possibility of that particular demand. For example, for demand of zero, we multiply $0, −$5000, −$10,000, −$20,000, and −$25,000 by .05. For a demand of 5000 units, we multiply $0, $10,000, $5,000, $0, −$5000, and −$10,000 by .15. We repeat this process for each demand. The results are shown in Table 22.

Table 22 shows that the optional supply level is 15,000 units, because the total of the 15,000-unit stock level column is greatest, $18,750. Table 22 also indicates that if we wish to reduce risk by ordering only 10,000 units, on the average this avoidance of risk will cost us approximately

TABLE 22   Conditional Profit and Loss Chart in Relation to Order Frequency (Dollars)

Possible Demand	Possible Supply × Order Frequency					
	0	5,000	10,000	15,000	20,000	25,000
0	0	−250	−500	−750	−1,000	−1,250
5,000	0	1,500	750	0	−750	−1,500
10,000	0	3,000	6,000	4,500	0	1,500
15,000	0	3,000	6,000	9,000	7,500	3,000
20,000	0	1,500	3,000	4,500	6,000	5,250
25,000	0	500	1,000	1,500	2,000	2,500
	0	9,250	16,250	18,750	13,750	9,500

$2500 ($18,750 − $16,250 = $2500). If we order 20,000 units in the hope of receiving that many orders, this gamble will cost us, on average, $5000 ($18,750 − $13,750 = $5000).

MATHEMATICAL VALUE OF PERFECT INFORMATION

In the previous example, by using a past order frequency distribution, we determined that on average we maximize profit by supplying 15,000 units. Note that this figure applies to only that example. But what if we could have a market survey conducted that could advise us with 100 percent accuracy of the exact level of demand for a particular item to be imported? What would be the maximum value of this information?

To find out, first we must realize that the overall percentages of order frequency will not change from the figures shown in Table 20. That is, for a particular item, there is a 5 percent chance that the quantity demanded will equal zero, a 15 percent chance that the quantity demanded will equal 5000 units, and so on. Second, we must keep in mind exactly how much profit we would make if we stocked the proper number of units to meet the demand, no more and no less. Table 23 reflects the profits that would be realized under each condition.

However, since we know how often each payoff can occur, we can calculate the average value of balancing supply exactly with demand. This calculation is shown in Table 24. Table 24 shows that with perfect information the average value is $25,000. Table 22 indicates that with no market information at all the optimal profit is $18,750. Therefore,

TABLE 23 Profit When Supply Equals Demand

Demand D	Supply S	Profit = S × $2
0	0	$0
5,000	5,000	$10,000
10,000	10,000	$20,000
15,000	15,000	$30,000
20,000	20,000	$40,000
25,000	25,000	$50,000

TABLE 24 Average Value When Supply Equals Demand

Profit P	Frequency F	P × F
$0	.05	$0
$10,000	.15	$1,500
$20,000	.30	$6,000
$30,000	.30	$9,000
$40,000	.15	$6,000
$50,000	.05	$2,500
		Total = $25,000

the maximum that a decision maker should pay for this perfect information is the difference between these two figures, or $6250.

SUMMARY

In this chapter we became familiar with some basic principles related to the value of information. The first principle simply states that the more important the decision is to the future of the organization, the more valuable or important is information needed to reach the right decision.

We reviewed the concept of examining potential extreme consequences resulting from a decision. If the extreme consequences of a decision could have only a minor impact (either good or bad), then a great deal of effort should not be expended in gathering information before a decision is made. If the extreme consequences could have a major impact on the future, then considerable information gathering is appropriate. This general rule must take into account the controls imposed on the outcome of the decision once it has been reached. The value of information is less when the level of control is low than when it is high.

We discussed the difference between quantifiable and nonquantifiable opportunity costs. Quantifiable opportunity costs can be identified as having a particular dollar value. Nonquantifiable opportunity costs cannot be identified with any accuracy as having a specific dollar value.

We emphasized the importance of adopting a successful decision-making strategy. We recommended observing both winning and losing strategies of people in similar decision-making circumstances. Then it is easy to emulate the winning strategy. Caution must be exercised to identify hidden factors which may influence an individual's strategy. The most common hidden factor is time.

We concluded this chapter with an example of how to use historical information as a guide in maximizing future profits. The actual numbers are not important, but what cannot be overemphasized is the need to have a historical data base. Although recordkeeping often is seen as a waste of time, this is not necessarily true. In deciding which records to keep and which to throw away, the critical question is, how will these data be used in the future? If there is no use for the data, do not keep the records. For data that is applicable, we presented a method to evaluate numerically the dollar value of obtaining additional information.

Chapter 11

Utility Theory

INTRODUCTION

The basic concept of utility theory is quite similar to that of risk and commitment discussed in Chapter 2. In utility theory there are two types of decision maker: risk-averting and risk-taking individuals. It is difficult to emulate a winning decision-making strategy because one unknown factor is the decision maker's tendency to take or avoid risks. To make it even more complicated, the individual's tendency changes as various factors relating to the decision change.

To illustrate, we offer the following examples.

Example 1

Assume that you are out to lunch with two acquaintances. One suggests flipping a coin to decide who will pay the total bill. Each person has had a lunch costing approximately $5, so the most you can gain is $5 and the most you can lose is $10. Should you agree to flip a coin or

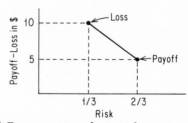

Figure 46 Indifference curve for a risk averter.

suggest that the group simply divide the bill? You should weigh a number of factors, including how much money you have with you, how honest your lunch partners are, and how long you must wait for the next payday. Regardless of the number of considerations, the factors will vary for each individual at the table. Figure 46 is a graphical illustration of the risk and payoffs in this situation. This figure shows that you have a 2:3 chance of winning $5 and a 1:3 chance of losing $10. If you are equally willing to take a chance or not take a chance (you are indifferent), then your personal preference falls on the line in Figure 46 that joins these two points.

Example 2

Assume that you are having lunch with the same acquaintances and someone in the restaurant suggests that the 100 diners there join a lottery and everyone throw in 5 cents. Thus as a result of the lottery, one diner would have lunch paid for by the group. Would you risk 5 cents to win a $5 meal with the odds 1:100 against you? Quite possibly you would take the chance, even though you knew that the odds were strongly against you. Why? The reason is that the investment is relatively insignificant. Figure 47 reflects this situation.

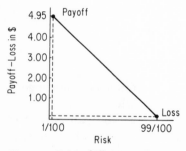

Figure 47 Indifference curve for a risk taker (not to scale). Note that the potential payoff is $4.95, since you must subtract the $.05 investment.

Note that your chances of winning in Figure 46 are much greater than in Figure 47. This is reflected by the reversed positions of the loss and payoff points in relation to which has the greater chance of occurring. You choose to take a risk based on two factors: the chance of a payoff or loss and the investment required.

Example 3

One other factor may influence your decision to take or avoid a risk. Reviewing Figures 46 and 47, you will note that in Figure 46 the chance of a loss is smaller than the chance of a gain, whereas in Figure 47 a payoff has a smaller chance of occurring than a loss. If you take a risk when the potential for payoff is greater than the potential for loss (Figure 46), then you may be considered a risk averter. If you take a risk when the potential for loss is greater than the potential for gain (Figure 47), then you may be considered to be a risk taker. Most people swing from one position to the other, depending on the stakes and risks entailed.

To illustrate, consider Example 2 and assume that someone in the restaurant suggests that the 100 diners join in a lottery and everyone draw a number from a hat. After the numbers have been chosen, a wheel is spun. The person whose number is selected must buy lunch for everyone. This risk indifference curve is shown in Figure 48.

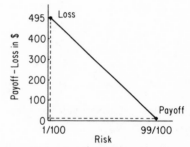

Figure 48   Indifference curve for a high-risk averter (not to scale). Note that the potential loss is $495 since you must subtract the $5 you owe for your own meal.

Would you be interested in such a gamble? Looking at Figure 48, you see that this situation is attractive to a risk averter, because the chance of loss is much smaller than the chance of gain. But the loss is much greater than the win.

We cannot answer this question for you, for each person views the situation relative to his or her particular circumstances. The only purpose of this example is to point out that different people and companies take different approaches to risk. A large company or wealthy individual can absorb a greater loss and so can take greater chances than a smaller investor. Therefore, the smaller investor often cannot take the chance, regardless of how attractive it is. The third factor that influences the decision maker relates to the value of the resources involved.

VALUE (OR UTILITY) OF RESOURCES

One of the most important considerations for a decision maker is the resources available. It is quite possible that any one of us might take a chance in Examples 1 and 2 and avoid taking a chance in Example 3, simply because of the magnitude of the potential loss. A wealthy person, considering $500 to be an insignificant amount, might not hesitate to gamble in Example 3.

This consideration is relevant in the business world as well as in our personal lives, with both individual and corporate decisions. Thus some companies can take far greater risks than others. If the extreme consequence is unfavorable, it is possible for the company to recover. See Figure 49.

Figure 49   Loss-payoff variable.

Figure 49 illustrates graphically the fact that, for any fixed investment, there is a potential for either a small payoff or loss or a much larger payoff or loss. This idea is illustrated on a limited scale by Figures 46 through 48. In each case you stand to win $5. However, in one case you could lose 5 cents whereas in another you could lose $495. This difference in potential loss obviously is related to the probability of each loss occurring. But an average wage earner may be quite reluctant to risk $495 just to win $5.

The same principle holds in business. A small investor may shy away from an investment with a potentially high payoff when it has a high potential for loss also. This may explain the fact that large corporations tend to spend lots of money on research whereas most small companies do not. It is not that small companies fail to appreciate the long-range benefits of research. Rather, they recognize the large investment involved and know that long-term payoffs will not help them much if they go out of business owing to a lack of working capital. One example of this principle occurs in the oil industry.

Example 4

Assume that it costs $100,000 to drill an oil well in search of an oil field. Further, assume that even with the best scientific equipment there is only a 1:100 chance that you will find oil by drilling for it. If you do find oil, the average value of a field is $12,500,000. To carry this example a little further, assume that after working for 20 years you have paid off the mortgage on your home, and its market value is $100,000. Now, should you sell your house and finance an oil drilling venture?

To answer this question, it is possible to approach the problem mathematically. For example, your chances of being successful are 1:100; so you simply assume that of 100 wells drilled only 1 is successful. Therefore, the total cost is 100 × $100,000 = $10,000,000. The average payoff for one strike is $12,500,000, so this looks like a great opportunity, right? Wrong! If you had the capital to explore 100 locations, it might be a great venture. But since you can drill only one well, the chances are still 100:1 that you will end up broke. Maybe this is the reason why so few people liquidate their life savings and take high-risk, high-payoff gambles and why large companies (such as oil companies) appear to prosper.

LOSS VERSUS PAYOFF

The oil-drilling example leads us to further discussion of Examples 1, 2, and 3. Would a wealthy individual or a large business repeatedly take any of these gambles? The answer is "No!" The reason is that, given the law of averages, someone who repeatedly takes any of these risks will break even. A company does not want to break even; it wants to make a profit.

Example 1 has a normalized profit-and-loss profile as follows:

$$\text{Normalized loss} = \text{potential loss} \times \text{risk}$$
$$= \$10 \times \tfrac{1}{3} = \$3.33$$
$$\text{Normalized payoff} = \text{potential payoff} \times \text{risk}$$
$$= \$5 \times \tfrac{2}{3} = \$3.33$$

Example 2 has this normalized profit-and-loss profile:

$$\text{Normalized loss} = \text{potential loss} \times \text{risk}$$
$$= \$0.05 \times \tfrac{99}{100} = \$0.0495$$
$$\text{Normalized payoff} = \text{potential payoff} \times \text{risk}$$
$$= \$4.95 \times \tfrac{1}{100} = \$0.0495$$

Example 3 has this normalized profit and loss profile:

$$\text{Normalized loss} = \text{potential loss} \times \text{risk}$$
$$= \$495 \times \tfrac{1}{100} = \$4.95$$
$$\text{Normalized payoff} = \text{potential payoff} \times \text{risk}$$
$$= \$5 \times \tfrac{99}{100} = \$4.95$$

In all three examples, the long-term normalized loss is equal to the long-term normalized payoff. This is fair to all concerned, but hardly profitable.

Using a rational decision-making method, first we try to determine both the potential payoff and the potential loss. Second, we try to find out the percentages of risk related to the payoff and the loss; these should add to unity. This is exactly what we did in Example 4. The calculations are as follows:

$$\text{Normalized loss} = \text{potential loss} \times \text{risk}$$
$$= \$100,000 \times \tfrac{99}{100} \times \$99,000$$
$$\text{Normalized payoff} = \text{potential payoff} \times \text{risk}$$
$$\$12,400,000 \times \tfrac{1}{100} = \$124,000$$

Clearly, this type of venture normally results in a payoff for the investor. This is illustrated by Figure 50.

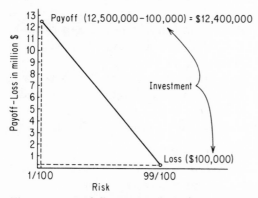

Figure 50   Indifference curve for a risk-prone oil well venture.

Note that this venture still has a greater chance of a loss than of payoff, which is similar to Figure 47. Does this mean that someone who enters into this type of venture is a risk taker? Not necessarily. Another factor that must be considered is possible long-term gain to be achieved by taking this risk a number of times.

CHAIN RISK

Still another factor to consider when you are pondering whether to get involved in a risky venture is *chain risk*. Chain risk relates to determining whether more risk is entailed than the basic problem would indicate at first.

Your original assessment of risk may be correct, but there may exist an additional risk that has not been taken into account. Refer to Example 4. Assume that the oil well is to be drilled in a foreign nation in which there is a 50:50 chance of a revolution resulting in the nationalization of all oil property. If you have the resources to drill a number of times, should you?

Prior to making any calculations, you must evaluate the impact of this new secondary risk. You recognize that this secondary risk will affect your chances for a payoff and for a loss. The original chances of success were 1:100. Now they are half that, ½:100, or .5:100. If this is the possibility of a payoff, then the chance of a loss must be 99½:100, in order for total risk to equal unity.

The values of the potential loss and payoff have not changed. However, when you include the revised risk factors in the normalized calculations, you find the following:

$$\text{Normalized loss} = \text{potential loss} \times \text{risk}$$
$$= \$100,000 \times \frac{99.5}{100} = \$99,500$$
$$\text{Normalized payoff} = \text{potential payoff} \times \text{risk}$$
$$= (12,500,000 - 100,000) \times \frac{.5}{100} = \$62,000$$

Figure 51 shows that the additional risk does not change either how much you must invest in this venture or how much you will gain if a payoff is made. In effect, the additional risk reduces the chances of a win by 50 percent and increases the chance of a loss by an equal amount.

As expected, the normalized loss has increased slightly, but the normalized payoff has been cut in half. Therefore, what looked like a promising investment for a company that could afford to play the high-risk, high-payoff game suddenly becomes a losing proposition, regardless of the capital resources available. This does not mean that for any given venture you cannot win. It simply means that for this type of investment you end up losing in the long run.

Remember that chain risk (or multiple risk) is not additive. You *mul-*

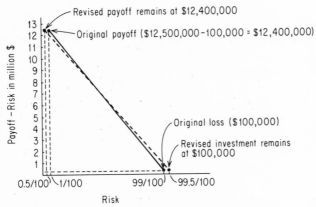

Figure 51 A single link in a chain-risk indifference curve.

tiply individual risks to form the total risk potential. A simple example is the flipping of a coin. Heads come up 50 percent of the time, and tails 50 percent of the time. What is the chance of getting heads three times in a row? It is $.5 \times .5 \times .5 = .125$, or 12.5 percent. Therefore, if someone repeatedly bets you $1 to $0.10 that you cannot get three heads in a row, take the bet, because you will win in the long run. To illustrate,

$$\text{Normalized payoff} = \text{potential payoff} \times \text{risk}$$
$$= \$1 \times (.5)(.5)(.5) = \$1(0.125) = \$0.125$$
$$\text{Normalized loss} = \text{potential loss} \times \text{risk}$$
$$= \$0.10 \times (1 - .125) = \$0.10 \, (.875) = \$0.875$$

If you added the risk factors, you would end up with $.5 + .5 + .5 = 1.5$, which means you would lose 150 percent of the time. This is obviously incorrect. But would this fact be so obvious if the possibility related to a small percentage? For example, what is the chance of rolling a given number, on a fair die, three times in a row? It is $(\frac{1}{6})(\frac{1}{6})(\frac{1}{6})$, or a 1:216 chance, *not* $\frac{1}{6} + \frac{1}{6} + \frac{1}{6}$.

Also remember that the total risk must equal unity. This statement is true for certain types of venture and may not be relevant in a real-life situation. For example, in some ventures a partial payoff may be feasible, which adds another dimension to the problem.

To illustrate this point, consider the oil-drilling venture with some additional assumptions. Assume that if you do strike oil, it takes 2 years to realize the $12,400,000 payoff. If you are concerned about the secondary risk of the oil fields being nationalized, then you should include that common variable which can make or break many investment situations, time. Assuming that 1 in 100 attempts to find oil are successful, how long will it take to find oil? Will the first well or the hundredth well pay off, and how long will it take to drill 100 wells? Say it takes 1 year to drill 100 wells. And for lack of any better information, assume that the fiftieth well will be successful, while a pessimist assumes the hundredth well will be successful. For this example, though, assume that it is the fiftieth. Also assume that the payoff is evenly distributed from the time oil is found until 2 years has passed.

Given all these assumptions, you can calculate how much time must pass before you break even:

$$\text{Time before success} = \frac{50 \text{ wells}}{100 \text{ wells}} \times \left(\frac{1 \text{ yr}}{\text{all wells}} \right) = 6 \text{ months}$$

$$\text{Funds invested} = 50 \text{ wells} \times \$100{,}000 = \$5{,}000{,}000$$

$$\text{Payoff rate} = \frac{\$12{,}500{,}000}{24 \text{ months}} = \$520{,}833 \text{ monthly}$$

$$\text{Breakeven payoff time} = \frac{5{,}000{,}000}{520{,}833} = 9.6 \text{ months}$$

$$\text{Total payoff time} = \text{Time to make strike} + \text{payoff time}$$
$$= 6 + 9.6 = 15.6 \text{ months}$$

These calculations indicate that under normalized conditions you can start to make money if you find oil and the oil fields are not nationalized before 15.6 months. To see how this relates to both the pessimistic and optimistic viewpoint, perform the analysis under both conditions.

The optimistic viewpoint requires the following calculations:

$$\text{Time before success} = \tfrac{1}{100} \times 1 \text{ yr} = 3.6 \text{ days}$$

$$\text{Funds invested} = 1 \text{ well} \times \$100{,}000 = \$100{,}000$$

$$\text{Payoff rate} = \$520{,}883 \text{ monthly} = \$17{,}361 \text{ daily}$$

$$\text{Breakeven payoff time} = \frac{100{,}000}{17{,}361} = 5.76 \text{ days}$$

$$\text{Total pay-off time} = 3.6 + 5.76 = 9.36 \text{ days} = .31 \text{ month}$$

For the pessimistic viewpoint, the calculations are as follows:

$$\text{Time before success} = \tfrac{100}{100} \times 1 \text{ yr} = 12 \text{ months}$$

$$\text{Funds invested} = 100 \text{ wells} \times \$100{,}000 = \$10{,}000{,}000$$

$$\text{Payoff rate} = \$520{,}833 \text{ monthly}$$

$$\text{Breakeven payoff time} = \frac{10{,}000{,}000}{520{,}833} = 19.2 \text{ months}$$

$$\text{Total payoff time} = 12 + 19.2 = 31.2 \text{ months}$$

Now you can look at the data and decide whether you feel optimistic or pessimistic. Also you could plot the three points calculated and develop a breakeven line identifying the number of months you would have to be in operation in order to break even after drilling any number of wells. This is illustrated by Figure 52.

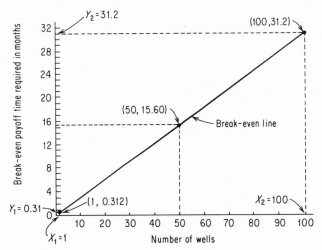

Figure 52 Number of wells versus Breakeven Requirements.

The mathematically inclined will recognize Figure 52 as defining a linear equation

$$Y = mx + i$$

where Y = months
m = slope of the line
X = number of wells
i = Y intercept, that point where $X = 0$

To find the equation for this line, first determine the slope:

$$m = \frac{Y_2 - Y_1}{X_2 - X_1} = \frac{31.2 - .31}{100 - 1} = \frac{30.89}{99} = .312$$

Then, by using point (X_2, Y_2), find the Y intercept:

$$Y = mX + i$$
$$31.2 = .312\,(100) + i$$
$$0 = i$$

Thus

$$Y = .312X$$

or, to say it in words, the breakeven point (in months) equals .312 times the number of wells drilled. With this formula you can plug in any number of wells or months and find the related value. As an example, suppose you believe the well will not be nationalized for at least 1 year. You can plug in 12 for Y and find the number of wells that you can drill before striking oil while still breaking even:

$$Y = .312X$$

or

$$X = \frac{Y}{.312} = \frac{12}{.312} = 38.46, \text{ or 49 wells}$$

CONTINUOUS INVESTMENT

In the previous discussion it is assumed that once you hit a well, you do not drill any new ones. However, this may not be realistic, for the investor may know that there is a 1:100 chance of making a strike. The same odds are reflected by 10:1000, and it is possible that the first 10 test sights may be successful. If this is the situation you face, then the revised calculations for the optimistic viewpoint are as follows (X is the number of months in operation):

$$\text{Time before success} = \tfrac{1}{100} \times 1 \text{ yr} = 3.6 \text{ days} = .12 \text{ month}$$
$$\text{Funds invested} = 100\,\frac{\text{wells}}{\text{yr}}\;\frac{1\text{ yr}}{12\text{ months}}\;\frac{\$100,000}{\text{well}}\,X$$
$$= \$833,333X$$
$$\text{Payoff rate} = \$520,833.33 \text{ monthly}$$
$$\text{Total payoff} = \$520,833X$$

Note that both the total funds invested and total payoff are related to the number of months in operation. Also the investment rate exceeds the payoff rate. How can this be true? It is true because this artificial example set the investment rate over a 1-year period and the payoff rate over a 2-year period. This example illustrates the danger of making calculations based on final dollar values without taking into consideration time, or cash flow in this case. All this may indicate that the longer you operate, the greater your chance of losing. This holds for the chance of losing during the first year but not for that of the second and subsequent years, because the payoff doubles since two oil wells are producing during the second and subsequent years and so the payoff rate doubles, too. See Table 25 and Figure 53.

TABLE 25   Investment and Payoff Rates with Total Profit

| Time (Years) | Investment | | Payoff | | Total Profit ($000) |
	Rate ($)	Total ($000)	Monthly Rate ($)	Total ($000)	
1	833,333	10,000	520,833	6,250	−3,750
2	833,333	20,000	1,041,666	18,750	−1,250
3	833,333	30,000	1,041,666	31,250	1,250
4	833,333	40,000	1,041,666	43,750	3,750
5	833,333	50,000	1,041,666	56,250	6,250

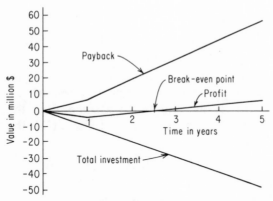

Figure 53   Investment, payoff, and profit curves.

These data reflect the optimistic viewpoint. Under similar circumstances, what would the pessimistic viewpoint look like? The following calculations apply when the hundredth well is successful (X = number of months in operation beyond 12):

$$\text{Time before success} = {}^{100}\!/_{100} \times 1 \text{ yr} = 12 \text{ months}$$
$$\text{Funds invested} = (\$100,000)(100) + \$833,333X$$
$$= \$10,000,000 + \$833,333X$$

Payoff rate = $520,833 monthly
Total payoff = $520,833X

These data reveal that the only difference between the optimist and pessimist is that the pessimist assumes operation continues a full year before oil is discovered. Since this extra year of operation costs $10,000,000, you can easily determine the breakeven point by calculating the difference between the investment and payoff rates: $1,041,666 − $833,333 = $208,333 monthly. To find the additional payoff time, you divide $10,000,000 by $208,333 per month to get 48 additional months, or a total of almost 7 years before you break even.

This is quite different from the data reflected by Figure 52. Are there other variables? You bet! For example, you could slow down the investment rate. You could drill until you made a strike and not drill again until the profits from the first strike pay for additional drillings, and so on.

SUMMARY

In this chapter we pointed out that the usefulness (or utility) or even the most desirable consequences are not the same for all decision makers. Although a particular result may be desired by more than one individual, the risk, the financial investment required, the value of resources, and the timing of the decision affect each decision maker differently. This is due to her or his unique circumstances, which often are not obvious to observers, who may only see the action taken or the results of the action taken.

We used the calculations simply to illustrate the impact of various factors on the final decision. Overlooking one of these factors could easily cause you to make a rational decision that would not have been made had all the factors been considered. These primary factors should influence your decision:

1. Availability of resources
2. Tendency (toward or away from) and identification of risk
3. Value (or utility) of resources
4. Timing

Although in our examples we could calculate the potential (or normalized) payoff and compare it with normalized loss, it is not always the case. This technique may be completely inappropriate for decisions involving personnel, organizational structure, work hours, pending modernization of facilities, and so on. However, the concept of chain risk is not associated with mathematical decisions only. For example, do not let the task of selecting the right person for a job mask the fact that another of your more valuable employees may resign if a particular person is chosen.

The advantage of examining end results cannot be stressed too much. If the worst-case condition occurs, then either you must be prepared for it or you should not take the risk to precipitate it. In making the best decision, you must ask yourself, Is it worth the risk? For example, in the oil-drilling example, is a 12.5 percent profit worth the risk, or should you look for a lower-risk venture to achieve this size profit? It might be possible to reduce the risk and increase the chances of success (or profit) simultaneously.

Chapter 12

Probability

INTRODUCTION

In many situations, before making a decision, a manager requests staff or subordinates to gather data for analysis. If the data make a clear-cut decision or choice obvious, then it is simple to pick a course of action. But most times the collected data are characterized by uncertainty. For example, if a decision must be made regarding the distribution of a product, it has to be based on only an estimate of the potential product consumption at the distribution points. If this consumption were known in advance, the decision would result in neither an overage nor a shortage at the distribution points. However, such detailed information is rarely known. Usually the data available to the manager are couched in terms of probability. In business, this is done for two reasons. First, exact data are not available. Second, the provider of the information, having stated that there is always a chance of the given data not matching real-life data, can never be accused of giving improper information. In business the second reason is referred to as job security.

Since a considerable amount of data is provided to a manager in terms of probability, he or she would be wise to understand it in order to properly utilize such information.

Probability theory involves no more than taking advantage of patterns that have been established from long-term, repeated occurrences of similar events. The most common example of a repeated occurrence is the flipping of a coin. We can visualize clearly that in the long run a fair coin will land heads half the time and tails half the time. But there is no way to accurately predict the outcome of a particular flip. The same principle holds when a decision is made regarding the probable distribution of a product. It may be possible to determine that product consumption will be above a certain level half the time and below that level half the time, but it is impossible to predict the exact consumption on a particular day.

INDEPENDENT PROBABILITY: GRAPHIC ILLUSTRATION

If two events are independent of each other, then the occurrence of one event has no affect on the occurrence of the other. This idea can be illustrated by tossing a coin. The outcome of the first toss has no impact on the outcome of the second toss. This principle holds true also for determining the probability of consumption of a product. If outside forces do not affect consumption, then consumption on one day will have no relation to consumption on the next day.

As an example of independent probability, consider that the probability of a bank teller making an error in giving change is 1 in 100 for any given week. What is the probability of a teller making an error for 2 weeks in a row? For 3 weeks in a row? For 4 weeks in a row? If you do not know how to evaluate these combined probabilities, how can you determine whether events are occurring that are so unusual that you suspect outside forces have influenced the outcome?

If the chance of an error is 1:100, or 1 percent, then we can identify the probability of occurrence as .01. Thus the probability of nonoccurrence is .99, because the total probability of occurrence and nonoccurrence must equal 100 percent, or 1. This is illustrated in Figure 54. The

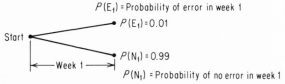

Figure 54   Probability of error in week 1.

following calculations are more easily understood with the assistance of these equivalencies:

$$P(E_1) = \text{probability of error in week 1}$$
$$P(N_1) = \text{probability of no error in week 1}$$
$$P(E_{1,2}) = \text{probability of error in weeks 1 and 2}$$
$$P(E_1, N_2) = \text{probability of error in week 1 and no error in week 2}$$
$$P(N_1, E_2) = \text{probability of no error in week 1 and error in week 2}$$
$$P(N_{1,2}) = \text{probability of no error in weeks 1 and 2}$$

$P(E_{1-4})$ = probability of error in weeks 1, 2, 3, and 4

$P(E_{1-3}, N_4)$ = probability of error in weeks 1, 2, and 3 and no error in week 4

$P(E_{1,2}, N_3, E_4)$ = probability of error in weeks 1 and 2, no error in week 3, and error in week 4

$P(E_{1,2}, N_{3,4})$ = probability of error in weeks 1 and 2 and no error in weeks 3 and 4

$P(E_1, N_2, E_{3,4})$ = probability of error in week 1, no error in week 2, and error in weeks 3 and 4

.
.
.

$P(N_{1-4})$ = probability of no error in weeks 1, 2, 3, and 4

What is the probability of an error for 2 weeks in a row? For 3 weeks? For 4 weeks? We can evaluate this diagrammatically by expanding Figure 54 to cover the particular time interval of interest. Let's start where the probability of an error in week 1 is $P(E_1) = .01$ and expand Figure 54 for 1 more week. The probability of an error in the second week $P(E_2)$ remains .01. However, if we consider this in conjunction with the first week's probability of .01, then the probability of an error for 2 weeks in succession is .01 times the first week's probability, or .01 $\times$ .01 = .0001. Thus the probability of no error occurring after the first week's error is .01 $\times$ .99 = .0099. Similar calculations can be done for the lower branch of Figure 54. The probability of no error in week 1 and an error in week 2 is $P(N_1, E_2) = .99 \times .01 = .0099$; likewise, the probability of no error in weeks 1 and 2 is $P(N_{1,2}) = .99 \times .99 = .9801$. This is illustrated in Figure 55.

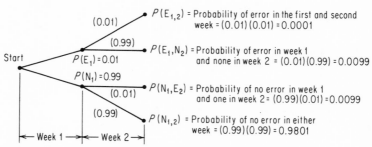

Figure 55 Probability of error in a two-week period.

A review of Figure 55 reveals some interesting facts. The total prob-
ability at the end of each week is unity. In the first week, $.01 + .99 = 1$. At the end of the second week the total probability is $.0001 + .0099 + .0099 + .9801 = 1$. This is logical because when all the probabilities
are added, they must account for 100 percent of the potential outcomes.
Also the probability of an error occurring in the first week only or in
the second week only is .0099. If we want to know the probability of one
error occurring within 2 weeks and we do not care during which week,
then we add $P(E_1, N_2)$ to $P(N_1, E_2)$ to find the combined probability:
$.0099 + .0099 = .0198$.

Figure 56 is Figure 55 expanded to a 4-week period. Some of the
nomenclature has been eliminated for clarity, but the subscripts follow
the same logic as displayed in Figures 54 and 55. Note that the total
probability at the end of each period still equals 1.

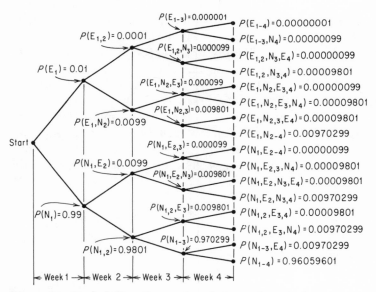

Figure 56   Probability of error in a four-week period.

Week 1 $\qquad\qquad\qquad P(E_1) + P(N_1) = 1$
$$.01 + .99 = 1$$

Week 2 $\qquad P(E_{1,2}) + P(E_1, N_2) + P(N_1, E_2) + P(N_{1,2}) = 1$
$$.0001 + .0099 + .0099 + .9801 = 1$$

Week 3 $P(E_{1-3}) + P(E_{1,2}, N_3) + P(E_1, N_2, E_3) + P(E_1, N_{2,3})$
$+ P(N_1, E_{2,3}) + P(N_1, E_2, N_3) + P(N_{1,2}, E_3) + P(N_{1-3}) = 1$

.000001 + .000099 + .000099 + .009801 + .000099
+ .009801 + .009801 + .970299 = 1

Week 4 $P(E_{1-4}) + P(E_{1-3}, N_4) + P(E_{1,2}, N_3, E_4) + P(E_{1,2}, N_{3,4})$
$+ P(E_1, N_2, E_{3,4}) + P(E_1, N_2, E_3, N_4) + P(E_1, N_{2,3}, E_4)$
$+ P(E_1, N_{2-4}) + P(N_1, E_{2-4}) + P(N_1, E_{2,3}, N_4)$
$+ P(N_1, E_{2-4}) + P(N_1, E_{2,3}, N_4) + P(N_{1,2}, E_{3,4})$
$+ P(N_{1,2}, E_3, N_4) + P(N_{1-3}, E_4) + P(N_{1-4}) = 1$

.00000001 + .00000099 + .00000099 + .00009801 + .00000099
+ .00009801 + .00009801 + .00970299 + .00000099
+ .00009801 + .00009801 + .00970299 + .00009801
+ .00970299 + .00970299 + .96059601 = 1

It is also possible by using Figure 56 to find the probability of zero, one, two, three, or four errors in a 4-week period:

A. Probability of no errors:

$$P(N_4) = .96059601$$

B. Probability of one or more errors:

$$1.00000000 - .96059601 = .03940399$$

C. Probability of one error:

$P(N_{1-3}, E_4) + P(N_{1,2}, E_3, N_4) + P(N_1, E_2, N_{3,4}) + P(E_1, N_{2-4})$
$= .00970299 + .00970299 + .00970299 + .00970299 = .03881196$

D. Probability of two errors:

$P(N_{1,2}, E_{3,4}) + P(N_1, E_2, N_3, E_4) + P(N_1, E_{2,3}, N_4) + P(E_1, N_{2,3}, E_4)$
$+ P(E_1, N_2, E_3, N_4) + P(E_{1,2}, N_{3,4}) = .00009801 + .00009801$
$+ .00009801 + .00009801 + .00009801 + .00009801 = .00058806$

E. Probability of three errors:

$P(N_1, E_{2-4}) + P(E_1, N_2, E_{3,4}) + P(E_{1,2}, N_3, E_4) + P(E_{1-3}, N_4)$
$= .00000099 + .00000099 + .00000099 + .00000099 = .00000396$

F. Probability of four errors:

$$P(E_{1-4}) = .00000001$$

G. Probability of less than four errors:

$$1.0000000 - .00000001 = .99999999$$

Two checks of these calculations should be made: Does item B equal items C + D + E + F, and does item G equal items A + C + D + E? These equalities should hold if no mathematical errors have been made, because the probabilities must total to unity. The equation B = C + D + E + F says that the probability of one or more errors is equal to the total of the probability of one error plus the probability of two errors plus the probability of three errors plus the probability of four errors. Substituting the numerical values yields

$$B = C + D + E + F$$
.03940399 = .03881196 + .00058806 + .00000396 + .00000001
.03940399 = .03940399

And it checks.

Does the probability of less than four errors equal the sum of the probabilities of zero, one, two, or three errors? Let's see:

$$G = A + C + D + E$$
.99999999 = .96059601 + .03881196 + .00058806 + .00000396
.99999999 = .99999999

INDEPENDENT PROBABILITY: MATHEMATICAL SOLUTION

The previous example is not meant to discourage anyone from utilizing independent probability theory. Rather, we wished to graphically illustrate how independent probabilities affect the overall probability when they occur in successive time frames. Fortunately, there is a shorter method, so we do not have to develop a chart each time we wish to evaluate independent probabilities. Imagine the size of the chart and the consequent calculations if we expanded Figure 56 to cover an entire year, or 52 weeks! What is the probability of no errors for an entire year?

Refer to Figure 56. The first part of the mathematical solution involves finding how often one could have zero, one, two, three, or four errors in a 4-week time frame. For example, to find the number of times one could have no errors in weeks 1, 2, 3, and 4, we simply look at the list on the right in Figure 56. In only one expression do we see N_{1-4}, so this happens once. Thus one can have zero, one, two, three, and four errors in a 4-week period 1, 4, 6, 4, and 1 times.

To find this mathematically, we use the following formulas:

$$C_N = \frac{t!}{N!(t - N)!}$$

or

$$C_N = \frac{t!}{N! + (t - N)!} \quad \text{if } N = t \text{ or } N = 0$$

where C_N = the number of combinations in which N errors appear
$\quad\quad N$ = the number of errors in a sequence
$\quad\quad t!$ = the number of time intervals of interest multiplied factorially

Any number multiplied factorially is that number times 1 less than the number, times 2 less than the number, times 3 less than the number, and so on, times 1. For example, 6 factorial is $6! = 6 \times 5 \times 4 \times 3 \times 2 \times 1 = 720$.

For Figure 54 the number of times one could have zero or one error is

$$C_0 = \frac{t!}{N! + (t - N)!} \quad\quad N = 0, t = 1$$
$$\quad\quad\quad\quad\quad\quad\quad\quad\quad\quad \text{Note: } N = 0$$
$$\quad = \frac{1!}{0! + (1 - 0)!} = 1$$

$$C_1 = \frac{t!}{N! + (t - N)!} \quad\quad N = 1, t = 1$$
$$\quad\quad\quad\quad\quad\quad\quad\quad\quad\quad \text{Note: } N = t$$
$$\quad = \frac{1!}{1! + (1 - 1)!} = 1$$

It is not possible to have N greater than t, because one cannot make more errors per time interval than there are time intervals.

For Figure 55 the number of times one could have zero, one, or two errors is

$$C_0 = \frac{t!}{N! + (t - N)!} \qquad\qquad N = 0, t = 2$$
$$\text{Note: } N = 0$$
$$= \frac{2 \times 1}{0! + (2 - 0)!} = 1$$

$$C_1 = \frac{t!}{N!(t - N)!} \qquad\qquad N = 1, t = 2$$

$$= \frac{2 \times 1}{1!(2 - 1)!} = 2$$

$$C_2 = \frac{t!}{N! + (t - N)!} \qquad\qquad N = 2, t = 2$$
$$\text{Note: } N = t$$
$$= \frac{2 \times 1}{2! + (2 - 2)!} = 1$$

For Figure 56 the number of times one could have zero, one, two, three, or four errors is

$$C_0 = \frac{4 \times 3 \times 2 \times 1}{0! + (4 - 0)!} \qquad\qquad N = 0, t = 4$$
$$\text{Note: } N = 0$$
$$= \frac{24}{4 \times 3 \times 2 \times 1} = 1$$

$$C_1 = \frac{4 \times 3 \times 2 \times 1}{1!(4 - 1)!} \qquad\qquad N = 1, t = 4$$

$$= \frac{24}{3 \times 2 \times 1} = 4$$

$$C_2 = \frac{4 \times 3 \times 2 \times 1}{2!(4 - 2)!} \qquad\qquad N = 2, t = 4$$

$$= \frac{24}{2 \times 2} = 6$$

$$C_3 = \frac{4 \times 3 \times 2 \times 1}{3!(4 - 3)!} \qquad\qquad N = 3, t = 4$$

$$= \frac{24}{3 \times 2 \times 1 \times 1} = 4$$

$$C_4 = \frac{4 \times 3 \times 2 \times 1}{4! + (4 - 4)!} \qquad\qquad N = 4, t = 4$$
$$\text{Note: } N = t$$
$$= \frac{24}{4 \times 3 \times 2 \times 1 + 0} = 1$$

The last part of the solution involves determining P_s, the probability of a particular sequence occurring. The formula is

$$P_s = [P(\text{N})^{t(\text{N})}][P(\text{E})^{t(\text{E})}]$$

In words, the probability of a sequence equals the probability of no error raised to number of times no error occurs, times the probability of an error raised to the number of times that an error occurs. It is clear that the number of time intervals with no errors $t(N)$ and the number of time intervals with an error $t(E)$ equal the total number of time intervals. For an example, see Figure 54. Then $P_s = P(E) = (.01)^1(.99)^0 = .01$ and $P_s = P(N) = (.99)^1(.01)^0 = .99$. For one interval, $t(N) + t(E) = 1 + 0$ or $0 + 1 = 1$.

For Figure 55:

$$P(E_{1,2}) = (.01)^2(.99)^0 = .0001 \qquad t(E) + t(N) = 2 + 0 = 2$$
$$P(E_1, N_2) = (.01)^1(.99)^1 = .0099 \qquad t(N) + t(E) = 1 + 1 = 2$$
$$P(N_1, E_2) = (.99)^1(.01)^1 = .0099 \qquad t(N) + t(E) = 1 + 1 = 2$$
$$P(N_{1,2}) = (.99)^2(.01)^0 = .9801 \qquad t(N) + t(E) = 2 + 0 = 2$$

For Figure 56:

$$P(E_{1-4}) = (.01)^4(.99)^0 = .00000001 \qquad t(E) + t(N) = 4 + 0 = 4$$
$$P(E_{1-3}, N_4) = (.01)^3(.99)^1 = .00000099 \qquad t(E) + t(N) = 3 + 1 = 4$$
$$P(E_{1,2}, N_{3,4}) = (.01)^2(.99)^2 = .00009801 \qquad t(E) + t(N) = 2 + 2 = 4$$
$$P(E_1, N_{2-4}) = (.01)^1(.99)^3 = .00970299 \qquad t(E) + t(N) = 1 + 3 = 4$$
$$P(N_{1-4}) = (.01)^0(.99)^4 = .96059601 \qquad t(E) + t(N) = 0 + 4 = 4$$

When these two pieces of information are combined, we can find mathematically the probability of any number of errors occurring in a particular period (see Figure 56):

A. The possibility of four errors equals the number of times one could have four errors, times the probability of a sequence with four errors:

$$P(4E) = C_0 \times P(E_{1-4}) = 1(.00000001) = .00000001$$

B. The possibility of three errors equals the number of times one could have three errors, times the probability of a sequence with three errors:

$$P(3E) = C_1 \times P(E_{1-3}, N_4) = 4(.00000099) = .00000396$$

C. The possibility of two errors equals the number of times one could have two errors, times the probability of a sequence with two errors:

$$P(2E) = C_2 \times P(E_{1,2}, N_{3,4}) = 6(.00009801) = .00058806$$

D. The possibility of one error equals the number of times one could have one error, times the probability of a sequence with one error:

$$P(1E) = C_3 \times P(E_1, N_{2-4}) = 4(.00970299) = .03881196$$

E. The possibility of no errors equals the number of times one could have no errors, times the probability of a sequence with no errors:

$$P(0E) = C_4 \times P(N_{1-4}) = 1(.96059601) = .96059601$$

F. The possibility of no errors for an entire year equals the number of times one could have no errors, times the probability of a sequence with no errors:

$$C_{52} = \frac{52!}{0! + (52 - 0)!} = \frac{52!}{52!} = 1$$
$$P(N_{1-52}) = (0.1)^0(.99)^{52} = .59296645$$
$$P(0E) = C_{52}P(N_{1-52}) = (1)(.59296645) = .59296645$$

These data may appear to be of little use. But clearly if a certain number of errors were made in a particular time frame, we would be able to determine whether this was within the norm or corrective action should be taken.

This example points out how such data could be useful in decision making. The concept applies to many other decisions in which data can be gathered and individual performance compared with what is expected. Some examples are machining errors, missed deadlines, use of sick leave, and late arrivals.

DEPENDENT PROBABILITY

If the probability of occurrence of one event is influenced by the occurrence or nonoccurrence of another event, then the probability of the second event depends on that of the first.

It is easiest to visualize this idea by drawing 1 card from a deck of 52. Before the card was drawn, there was a 26:52 chance, or a probability of .5, of the card being red and 26:52 chance, or a probability of .5, of the card being black. Once one card is removed from the deck, the chance of drawing the same-color card from the deck a second time is 25:51, or a probability of .49. The chance of a different-color card being chosen on the second draw is 26:51, or a probability of .51. The 25 is used because one card was removed from the original 26 cards of the color drawn, and 51 is the sum of the remaining 25 + 26 cards.

Now we give an example of a more work-related use of dependent probability. Assume we must make a decision related to the introduction of a new quality assurance (QA) procedure that promises to reduce the possibility of producing defective parts to 5 per 100 units. We do not expect the market to increase or decrease substantially, but we are interested in minimizing the number of defective parts. The problem with the new QA procedure is that it, too, entails a cost. The data for the number of defective parts are shown in Table 26.

TABLE 26   Defective Parts per 1000 Units Produced (Before Quality Assurance)

	Part					
	A	B	C	D	E	Total
Defectives	15	15	5	5	30	70
Nondefectives	185	235	95	45	370	930
Total	200	250	100	50	400	1000

Given the number of parts in each category, when total production is 1000 units, we can make some predictions regarding the probability of a particular part being a portion of the total production:

Part A $\qquad P = {}^{200}\!/_{1000} = .20$

Part B $\qquad P = {}^{250}\!/_{1000} = .25$

Part C $\qquad P = {}^{100}\!/_{1000} = .10$

Part D $\qquad P = {}^{50}\!/_{1000} = .05$

Part E $\qquad P = {}^{400}\!/_{1000} = .40$

The chance of a defect being found in any part produced is 70:1000, or a probability of .07. The probability of defective parts following the improved QA procedure is .05. With these data alone, we would favor the introduction of the QA procedure. But before we take this step, we would be wise to find the probability of defects being strongly tied to the production of a particular part:

Part A $\qquad P = {}^{15}\!/_{200} = .075$

Part B $\qquad P = {}^{15}\!/_{250} = .06$

Part C $P = \frac{5}{100} = .05$
Part D $P = \frac{5}{50} = .10$
Part E $P = \frac{30}{400} = .075$

A review of these data reveals that some parts have a high probability of being defective (.10) and others a relatively low probability of being defective (.05). This fact leads us to more questions. We should determine whether the new QA procedure can be applied to some parts and not to others. What is the cost of the new procedure per part? What is the cost of defective parts?

We could continue this example by providing dollar figures for each of the previous questions and then calculating profit or loss. However, the purpose of this example is not to practice mathematics. Rather, the point is that when faced with data which clearly indicate a course of action (such as .05 defectives versus .07), usually we should look more closely at the data. Once again, figures do not lie, but liars figure. The basic concepts of probability are essential to a more in-depth look.

To illustrate the information that can be drawn from a single table, we use Table 26 to derive data that may or may not be of considerable interest, depending on the decision to be made and our evaluation of the pertinence of the information. Say we wish to find the probability that any one defect in the total number of defects is associated with a particular part:

Part A $P = \frac{15}{70} = .21$
Part B $P = \frac{15}{70} = .21$
Part C $P = \frac{5}{70} = .07$
Part D $P = \frac{5}{70} = .07$
Part E $P = \frac{30}{70} = .43$

Or we may be interested in determining the probability that of the total items produced one particular part has a defect:

Part A $P = \frac{15}{1000} = .015$
Part B $P = \frac{15}{1000} = .015$
Part C $P = \frac{5}{1000} = .005$
Part D $P = \frac{5}{1000} = .005$
Part E $P = \frac{30}{1000} = .03$

Suppose we were able to use the improved QA procedures in the manufacture of part D. This decision could be justified by the fact that we found part D to have a higher probability of a defect than any other part. So the revised table would look like Table 27.

Table 26 shows a rate of 70 defective parts per 1000 units. Table 27 shows a rate of 67.5 defects per 1000 units. Is the reduction in defective parts reflected by [(5 − 2.5)/5]100, or 50 percent; by [(70 − 67.5)/

TABLE 27   Defective Parts per 1000 Units Produced (After Quality Assurance)

	Part					
	A	B	C	D	E	Total
Defectives	15	15	5	2.5	30	67.5
Nondefectives	185	235	95	47.5	370	932.5
Total	200	250	100	50	400	1000

70]100, or .036 percent; or by [(70 − 67.5)/1000]100, or .0025 percent? Many times data are presented so as to reflect the vested interest of the presentor. The salesperson attempting to sell the QA procedure is likely to boast a 50 percent reduction in defective parts. The existing QA manager (who may feel his or her job is threatened) may point out that .0025 percent improvement is hardly worth the risk of purchasing an untried procedure.

SUMMARY

In this chapter we did not purport to offer in-depth knowledge of the theories or mathematics in probability theory. We did distinguish, though, between two basic types of probability: independent and dependent.

The basic concept of independent probability can be illustrated by the flip of a coin. If we flip a fair coin 25 times and it comes up heads each time, the chance of getting a head on the next flip is still 50:50. The basic concept of dependent probability can be illustrated by drawing a card from a fair deck and not replacing the drawn card. We could draw a red card 25 times in a row, but the next time we draw a card, the chance of it being red is only 1:27.

When the data is given as probabilities, first we must determine whether they are independent or dependent. Second, we have to be extremely careful to know just what the data defines. Data can be accurate yet misleading when the person gathering and presenting it follows one line of logic and we follow another. This difference in perception can be intentional or nonintentional, but the results are the same: a poor decision will be made. I prefer to think that this difference is most likely the result of misunderstanding rather than deception. Nonetheless, misunderstanding can be even more dangerous than deception, because the parties involved in the decision making process are unaware that there is no meeting of the minds.

Here is an example of misunderstanding: A supervisor in a large corporation requests a new secretary to burn a copy of an important contract. The secretary says, "Pardon me?" The supervisor replies, "Burn it! Burn it!" *Burn it* is a common expression used in the office to mean "make a copy." But it was not familiar to the new employee, so a considerable amount of work went up in flames. If face-to-face communications can be so radically misinterpreted, obviously written work can be misinterpreted very easily, too. The use of numerical data is even more subject to misinterpretation unless the person preparing the data and the person reviewing it are operating from the same perspective.

Chapter **13**

Statistics

INTRODUCTION

To many managers, the word *statistics* can conjure up visions of massive charts, graphs, and numbers identified by strange symbols. Many times this perception is more true than false, because many statisticians tend to give managers more information than they really need to make decisions. This difficulty arises when the data preparer does not know its exact purpose and the individual examining the data is not specific or perhaps does not even know exactly what data he or she wants or should request.

The science of statistics has expanded so much that the average person can get lost easily in the terminology, definitions, and symbolism. But this does not prevent that person from utilizing this powerful tool. Just as you do not need a medical degree to take most prescription drugs, you do not need to be a statistician to use statistical data. However, with data as with prescription drugs, you must know whether to read the fine print or swallow on faith.

The information provided in this chapter only scratches the surface of statistics. But, armed with this information, you should be able to determine generally whether data fall into a category in which statistical analysis is appropriate.

RANDOM VARIABLES

A *random variable* can be thought of as a numerical value that fluctuates in no predictable manner. Let us return to the coin flipping example. When we flip a coin, we know it will land with either a head or a tail facing up, but we have no accurate way to predict which it will be for any one flip. The outcome of the first flip has absolutely no influence on those of subsequent flips.

Random variables are either discrete or continuous. A *discrete* random variable is a concrete number, for example, how many times a coin is flipped. It is never flipped 6½ times. One example of a *continuous* random variable is the definition of how tall an individual is. Height is subject to a number of variables. Did the person being measured wear shoes, socks, or a hat or have long hair? Was the measurement taken from the top of the hair, or was the hair compressed to the skull? How accurate was the measurement? To how many decimal points?

For our purposes we concentrate on discrete random variables. Thus we eliminate any question realted to interpretation of one piece of data. We concentrate, instead, on the analysis of a specific piece of data (number) and its relationship to the remaining pieces of data (numbers).

CENTRAL TENDENCY

Central tendency refers to the massing of data about a single numerical point. Perhaps the most common synonym is the *average*. This term is familiar to us from examination results in school. Many people are not as familiar with terms such as *mode, mean,* and *median.* Each term describes this massing of data, yet a misinterpretation of one of these terms could lead to an improper decision.

To clearly define these terms, we resort to an example. Assume that 20 students took an examination of 10 questions with the results shown in Table 28. The *average* grade is the *same* as the *mean* grade. For the data in Table 28, we add the total number of correct answers for each frequency and divide by the total number of grades:

TABLE 28   Examination Results

Number Correct	Frequency	Number Correct	Frequency
1	0	6	2
2	1	7	6
3	0	8	4
4	0	9	3
5	1	10	3
			Total = 20

Average = mean = μ

$$= \frac{2 + 5 + 2(6) + 6(7) + 4(8) + 3(9) + 3(10)}{20}$$

$$= \frac{150}{20} = 7.5 \text{ correct}$$

The *mode* is simply the result that occurred with the highest frequency. For the data in Table 28, the mode is 7 correct answers.

The *median* is the number that occupies a position midway between the extremes. For example, in Table 28, the median is

$$\text{Median} = \frac{2 + 10}{2} = \frac{12}{2} = 6 \text{ correct}$$

Therefore, with one set of data, we can find three unique descriptions of central tendency, each with its own applications, depending on the use of the data. For example, a student who had only five correct answers might prefer to call it one less correct answer than the median score rather than reveal that only one student had fewer correct answers.

STANDARD DEVIATION

The standard deviation for a set of data defines the variability of the data. For two sets of data with the same mean, the standard deviation identifies the tendency of the data points to cluster about or spread away from the mean. Figure 57 shows two sets of data which have the same mean. But in curve *A* data are clustered closer to the mean than in curve *B*.

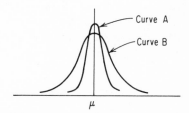

Figure 57 Two curves with the same mean but with different standard deviations.

166   Chapter Thirteen

The standard deviation, denoted σ (the Greek letter sigma), is used to define the limits within which a certain percentage of the data values lie. For a normal distribution, one standard deviation from the mean includes approximately 68 percent of all the values for the population. Two standard deviations include approximately 95 percent of the values, and three standard deviations include 99 percent of the values.

As an illustration, refer to the data in Table 28. We calculated the mean of those data to be 7.5. Assume that one standard deviation equals 1.5. Then 7.5 $\pm$ 1.5, or 68 percent of the correct answers for a large number of students taking this examination, should fall between 6 and 9. Thus 7.5 $\pm$ 2σ should contain 95 percent of the correct answers. Since it is impossible to have more correct answers on a test than there are questions, 95 percent of the answers should fall between 4.5 and 10. And 99 percent of the answers (7.5 $\pm$ 3σ) should fall between 3 and 10.

Note two things about this theoretical example. First, with a small sample size, any random data point will have a considerable impact on the data. Second, because this is true, the sample must be of sufficient size to make statistical analysis applicable. For example, suppose in a class of two students both scored 2 out of 10 correct. Should you conclude that both students did not understand the subject or that the test was too tough? Referring to Table 28, you note that one student had only two answers correct. This falls outside the 3σ limit. If the test sample is large enough for statistical analysis, you should investigate why the results for this student are so out of line compared with those of the rest of the class.

So how do you determine whether a sample is large enough? For the purposes of this text, you should have faith in your statistician. Although the mathematics is not complicated, it is beyond the scope of this chapter, and a review might well serve no useful purpose other than to make you aware that the number of data points in a sample determines the appropriateness of the statistical evaluation technique. The greater the data base, the more confidence you have in the results of an analysis. However, you should become familiar with the mathematical procedure used to find the standard deviation. The formula is as follows:

$$\text{Standard deviation} = \sigma = \sqrt{\frac{\Sigma_1^n (x - \mu)^2}{n}}$$

In words, the standard deviation equals the square root of the summation of the differences between each value x and the mean μ, squared, for every value from the first (1) to the last (n), divided by the total number of numbers n. To see how this works, let's calculate the standard deviation for the data in Table 28. Remember, $\mu = 7.5$.

n	Number Correct X	$x - \mu$	$(x - \mu)^2$
1	2	$2 - 7.5 = -5.5$	30.25
2	5	$5 - 7.5 = -2.5$	6.25
3	6	$6 - 7.5 = -1.5$	2.25
4	6	$6 - 7.5 = -1.5$	2.25
5	7	$7 - 7.5 = -0.5$	0.25
6	7	$7 - 7.5 = -0.5$	0.25
7	7	$7 - 7.5 = -0.5$	0.25
8	7	$7 - 7.5 = -0.5$	0.25
9	7	$7 - 7.5 = -0.5$	0.25
10	7	$7 - 7.5 = -0.5$	0.25
11	8	$8 - 7.5 = 0.5$	0.25
12	8	$8 - 7.5 = 0.5$	0.25
13	8	$8 - 7.5 = 0.5$	0.25
14	8	$8 - 7.5 = 0.5$	0.25
15	9	$9 - 7.5 = 1.5$	2.25
16	9	$9 - 7.5 = 1.5$	2.25
17	9	$9 - 7.5 = 1.5$	2.25
18	10	$10 - 7.5 = 2.5$	6.25
19	10	$10 - 7.5 = 2.5$	6.25
20	10	$10 - 7.5 = 2.5$	6.25
	$\Sigma x = 150$		$\Sigma(x - \mu)^2 = 69.00$

Thus

$$\text{Mean} = \frac{\text{sum of values}}{\text{no. of values}} = \frac{x}{n} = \frac{150}{20} = 7.5$$

$$\text{Standard deviation } \sigma = \sqrt{\frac{(x - \mu)^2}{n}} \cong \sqrt{\frac{69}{20}} = 1.9$$

If one standard deviation equals 1.9, then two standard deviations are $2 \times 1.9 = 3.8$, and three standard deviations are $3 \times 1.9 = 5.7$.

Therefore, if the students who took this test were typical of all students who might take it in the future, then 68 percent will score between 5.6 and 9.4 correct answers (7.5 ± 1.9), 95 percent will score between 3.7 and 10 correct answers (7.5 ± 3.8), and 99 percent will score between 1.8 and 10 correct answers (7.5 ± 5.7). By calculating the standard deviation, it is possible to more accurately evaluate individual performance as it relates to the total population. If you cannot predict the values that should fall within the expected range, then it will be impossible to determine whether a given result is acceptable.

CONTINUOUS PROBABILITY DISTRIBUTION

The continuous probability distribution comprises a full range of values that tend to mass about a mean value. The probability distribution tends to cluster about the mean value, as shown in Figure 57. The curves in Figure 57 typically are referred to as *normal*, or *bell-shaped*, *curves*. They represent the normal probability distribution of an infinite number of measurements. This normal curve is symmetric about an imaginary vertical line that passes through the mean (μ). Thus the height of the curve is the same if you move equal distances to the left and to the right of the mean. The "tails" of the curve come closer and closer to the horizontal axis, but never reach it. The curve never touches the horizontal line, since the area under the curve represents the probability of any one value being part of the overall population. The curve never touches the horizontal because there is always a remote chance that a particular value will be very remote from the mean. The balanced bell-shaped curve simply indicates that there is an equal probability of a value being the same number of standard deviations above or below the mean. The total area under a normal curve equals 1, or 100 percent of the possible values associated with the population.

Since each population studied has different values for the mean and standard deviation, the values related to a population are referred to as z values. One standard deviation (σ) is equal to one z value. Values higher than the mean values are considered positive z values whereas those less than the mean are considered negative z values. A given value at the mean is zero standard deviations from the mean, so the z value there equals zero. Figure 58 illustrates this concept.

To determine the z value for a given number, use the following formula:

$$z = \frac{x - \mu}{\sigma}$$

This says that the z value is found by subtracting the mean μ from the value x and dividing this figure by the standard deviation σ.

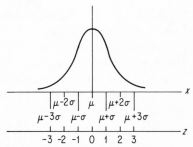

Figure 58   Relationship between σ and z values.

As an example, refer to the data in Table 28. Via previous calculations, we determined that the mean is 7.5 and the standard deviation is 1.9. For our purposes we want to determine the percentage of the population with 9 or 10 correct answers on a 10-question test. The z value is

$$z = \frac{x - \mu}{\sigma} = \frac{9 - 7.5}{1.9} = \frac{1.5}{1.9} = 0.79$$

This is illustrated by Figure 59.

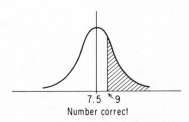

7.5 9
Number correct

Figure 59   Area of interest for student exam example.

Note that the area above 9 is shaded. This indicates that we are interested in the percent of the population with nine or more correct answers. Next refer to Table 29. Since we already found the z values to be 0.79, we look down the vertical z column to 0.7 and then move horizontally to the column entitled 0.09. This combination yields our z value of 0.79, which is found to be 0.2852. This number represents the area found between the mean and a standard deviation located 0.79z distant. This makes sense. We can see from Table 29 that as the z value gets smaller (or the distance from the mean gets smaller), the area under the curve becomes smaller. A look at the extremes of Table 29 reveals that if the distance from the mean is zero, then the area is zero. If the z value is as large as 3.09, then the area is close to 50 percent (49.90 percent) of that under the entire curve.

In our example, the z value is 0.2852. Thus the area between 7.5 and 9 is 28.52 percent of the total area under the curve. However, we want to find the percentage of area which is larger than a value of 9. Since each half of the standard curve is equal to 50 percent, we can calculate

TABLE 29   Area under the Standard Normal Curve

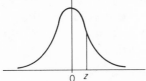

z	.00	.01	.02	.03	.04	.05	.06	.07	.08	.09
0.0	.0000	.0040	.0080	.0120	.0160	.0199	.0239	.0279	.0319	.0359
0.1	.0398	.0438	.0478	.0517	.0557	.0596	.0636	.0675	.0714	.0753
0.2	.0793	.0832	.0871	.0910	.0948	.0987	.1026	.1064	.1103	.1141
0.3	.1179	.1217	.1255	.1293	.1331	.1368	.1406	.1443	.1480	.1517
0.4	.1554	.1591	.1628	.1664	.1700	.1736	.1772	.1808	.1844	.1879
0.5	.1915	.1950	.1985	.2019	.2054	.2088	.2123	.2157	.2190	.2224
0.6	.2257	.2291	.2324	.2357	.2389	.2422	.2454	.2486	.2518	.2549
0.7	.2580	.2612	.2642	.2673	.2704	.2734	.2764	.2794	.2823	.2852
0.8	.2881	.2910	.2939	.2967	.2995	.3023	.3051	.3078	.3106	.3133
0.9	.3159	.3186	.3212	.3238	.3264	.3289	.3315	.3340	.3365	.3389
1.0	.3413	.3438	.3461	.3485	.3508	.3531	.3554	.3577	.3599	.3621
1.1	.3643	.3665	.3686	.3708	.3729	.3749	.3770	.3790	.3810	.3830
1.2	.3849	.3869	.3888	.3907	.3925	.3944	.3962	.3980	.3997	.4015
1.3	.4032	.4049	.4066	.4082	.4099	.4115	.4131	.4147	.4162	.4177
1.4	.4192	.4207	.4222	.4236	.4251	.4265	.4279	.4292	.4306	.4319
1.5	.4332	.4345	.4357	.4370	.4382	.4394	.4406	.4418	.4429	.4441
1.6	.4452	.4463	.4474	.4484	.4495	.4505	.4515	.4525	.4535	.4545
1.7	.4554	.4564	.4573	.4582	.4591	.4599	.4608	.4616	.4625	.4633
1.8	.4641	.4649	.4656	.4664	.4671	.4678	.4686	.4693	.4699	.4706
1.9	.4713	.4719	.4726	.4732	.4738	.4744	.4750	.4756	.4761	.4767
2.0	.4772	.4778	.4783	.4788	.4793	.4798	.4803	.4808	.4812	.4817
2.1	.4821	.4826	.4830	.4834	.4838	.4842	.4846	.4850	.4854	.4857
2.2	.4861	.4864	.4868	.4871	.4875	.4878	.4881	.4884	.4887	.4890
2.3	.4893	.4896	.4898	.4901	.4904	.4906	.4909	.4911	.4913	.4916
2.4	.4918	.4920	.4922	.4925	.4927	.4929	.4931	.4932	.4934	.4936
2.5	.4938	.4940	.4941	.4943	.4945	.4946	.4948	.4949	.4951	.4952
2.6	.4953	.4955	.4956	.4957	.4959	.4960	.4961	.4962	.4963	.4964
2.7	.4965	.4966	.4967	.4968	.4969	.4970	.4971	.4972	.4973	.4974
2.8	.4974	.4975	.4976	.4977	.4977	.4978	.4979	.4979	.4980	.4981
2.9	.4881	.4982	.4982	.4983	.4984	.4984	.4985	.4985	.4986	.4986
3.0	.49865	.4987	.4987	.4988	.4988	.4989	.4989	.4989	.4990	.4990

the area under the curve from 9 up by subtracting 0.2852 from 0.5000, to get 0.2148. This indicates that 21.48 percent of the population is represented by the area shaded in Figure 59. Or, in the long run, we expect 21.48 percent of the students who take that particular test to score 9 or 10 correct answers.

To ensure that this concept is clear, we present three examples to illustrate the mathematics of how to use Table 29 and apply the continuous probability.

Example 1

You manage a chain of small variety stores, and over the years you have determined the average gross sales per week to be $5000. Analyzing data from the entire chain, you also find that one standard deviation is equal to $1000. Further assume that profit is directly proportional to sales and that when sales drop below $3500, the stores' fixed costs make it unprofitable to operate. What are the chances that any given store will operate at a sales level below $3500 in a particular week?

Assuming that the data yield a standard distribution curve, you should sketch a bell-shaped curve and label the mean, the standard deviations, and the z values. The z value for $3500 is $(3500 - 5000)/1000$, or -1.5. Figure 60 shows a sketch of this example with the shaded area being the area of interest.

Table 29 reveals that a z value of 1.5 is equal to 0.4332. Table 29 can be used for either negative or positive z values; a $-z$ indicates that the value you are working with is below $(-)$ the mean value, $+z$ is above $(+)$ the mean value. Here .4332 represents the area under the curve in Figure 60 from $-1.5z$ to the mean. To find the area of the shaded por-

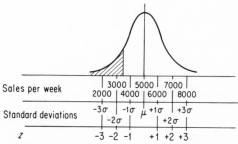

Figure 60 Area of interest for sales volume examples.

tion, we must subtract .4332 from .5000, to get .0668. Therefore, the chance that a given store will operate at a sales level below $3500 in a particular week is 6.68 percent. If a given store operates below this level for more than 6.68 percent of the time, then you certainly should investigate why.

Example 2

You are considering taking on a new job, a sales position with a salary based primarily on commission. Your present job is a salaried position, set at $28,000 per year. You are told that the salary range for the new position is represented by a normal curve, with an average salary of $30,000 per year and a standard deviation of $5000. You have decided that if you can make $5000 more per year in the sales job, then you will change jobs.

What are the chances that you will earn at least $5000 more per year than in your present job? What are the chances that you will earn more than you presently do? What are the chances that you will earn less than you presently do?

In all cases in which you plan to analyze the area under a normal curve, first sketch the curve and label the areas of interest. For this example, the areas of interest are the mean, $30,000; the z value for your existing salary, ($28,000 − $30,000)/$5000 = $-.4z$; and the z value for your desired salary, ($28,000 + $5000 − $30,000)/$5000 = $.6z$. These values are sketched in Figure 61.

The first question is, What are the chances of your earning at least $5000 more per year than at your present job? To determine this prob-

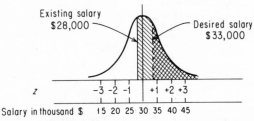

Figure 61   Area of interest for new job example.

ability, you must determine the area represented by the double crosshatched area in Figure 61. This area represents all the salaries which are $5000 above your present salary, or $33,000 per year. The z value has been calculated to be .6, so you look up the value of .6 in Table 29 and find a value of .2257. But remember that .2257 represents the area between the z value and the mean. To find the double crosshatched area, you subtract .2257 from .5000, to get .2743. So the chances that you will earn at least $5000 more per year than at your present position are 27.43 percent.

The second question is, What are the chances that you will earn more than you presently do? Since currently you earn $28,000 and the z value for that figure is $-.4$, you are interested in the area to the right of $z = -.4$. Table 29 reveals that the area associated with $z = .4$ is .1554. This represents the area between $z = -0.4$ and the mean. However, to this figure you must add all the area to the right of the mean. Since the area on each half of the curve is equal to .5000, you add .1554 to .5000, to arrive at .6554. Thus you have a 65.54 percent chance of having your salary increased.

The third and final question is, What are the chances that your salary will be decreased? Since the total area under the curve equals 1.0000, you find this figure by subtracting the area on the right side of $z = -.4$ (which you just found) from 1.0000, to get .3446. So you have a 34.46 percent chance of earning a smaller salary than you presently do.

Should you take the job? That depends on the other factors involved in making a change, which certainly would include your confidence in your ability to be a successful salesperson and your personal avoidance or nonavoidance of risk. But regardless of your final decision, certainly you benefit by being aware of the mathematical pros and cons of your decision.

Example 3

You are a manager in a large organization. You are reviewing some personal records for the previous year regarding the number of hours that various employees have been away from work owing to sickness. You have records indicating that the sick leave taken varies widely from 0 to 500 hours. Reviewing some of the longer absences, you find that many are due to serious illnesses or accidents. However, some high-rate users were not known to have any illnesses other than routine colds and dental appointments. If you decide to investigate the reasons of the high-rate users, where should you make the cutoff between high users and excessive users?

One method is to statistically analyze data and group users by category. The categories could be (1) low-use area, (2) normal-use area, (3) slightly high-use area, (4) suspicious-use area, and (5) mandatory investigation area. In actual practice, you could analyze the sick leave data as described earlier in this chapter. Assume that the analysis shows that the average use of sick leave is 2 weeks (80 hours) per year with a standard deviation of 40 hours. Then you should sketch a standard distribution curve and label the areas of interest. Figure 62 is a typical sketch.

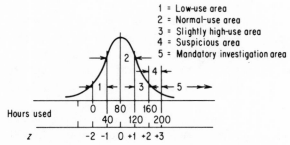

Figure 62   Area of interest for sick-leave example.

Figure 62 indicates that area 2 represents the normal-use rate and extends from $z = +1$ to $z = -1$. Table 29 indicates that $z = 1$ represents .3413, so the area from $z = +1$ to $z = -1$ is twice .3413, or .6826. Hence area 2 accounts for 68.26 percent of the employees' sick leave records.

You could analyze each area individually. But assume for the time being that you will accept a low-use area (1) and a slightly high-use area (3) but would like to know the chances of an individual's sick leave use falling into the suspicious-use area (4) between $z = 2$ and $z = 3$. Table 29 shows that $z = 2$ yields .4772 and $z = 3$ yields .49865. Since you are working with only one side of the curve, $.49865 - .4772 = .02145$ is the area between $z = 2$ and $z = 3$. So there is a 2.145 percent chance that an individual will use between 160 and 200 hours of sick leave.

What are the chances that an individual will use more than 200 hours? To find out, subtract the value for $z = 3$, or .49865, from .50000. Hence area 5 is equal to .00135, or .135 percent of the total. It would be difficult for an employee to feel singled out for an investigation based on anything but facts when you confront that person with his or her individual record and which area it falls into.

This analysis is not 100 percent accurate, because Figure 62 is truncated at $z = -2$ and the area below this point is not accounted for. However, this type of error is insignificant when you simply use this procedure to ascertain which areas to investigate and which areas appear normal.

SUMMARY

By no stretch of the imagination should this chapter be considered the bible of statistics. We only scratched the surface of how statistics can be used to help make decisions. A true statistician would be much more thorough and compile a great deal more data for any of the areas covered. This tendency to amass lots of data is often the primary problem with requesting experts to conduct a statistical analysis. Many times, the data provided are not only voluminous but also riddled with explanations of a host of terms which are understood only by someone completely familiar with the statistical process.

Do not be frightened off by terms such as *correlation, hypothesis, bivarian population, regression, sampling techniques, tests of association, functional relationships, confidence intervals,* and so on. Although all these terms have definite functions in the detailed science of statistical analysis, normally they have no place in a report to a general manager. Even if the person providing you with statistical data may present them in such a complex manner that they are useless to you, do not give up on statistical data in general. A superior approach would be to advise your supplier of exactly what you want and how you want it presented.

Chapter 14

Conclusion

INTRODUCTION

We provided an overview of the factors involved in a management decision. The basic requirement of recognizing the necessity of a decision is obvious, but many an industrial decision has been made by someone who did not even recognize that he or she was doing so. An example is the manager who does not recognize that a problem exists and through lack of action fails to affect the solution of the problem. In this case, the manager's failure to act could be a very significant factor.

When the mushroom effect is a strong influence in an organization, this is the norm. The mushroom effect is the result of an individual being kept in the dark and fed a lot of bull. In many organizations the workers accuse management of using this technique, but in reality this technique also is used to keep management in the dark. After all, management that knew about everything being done in the company would be equally aware of the failures and the successes.

As a manager, you must be aware that this phenomenon exists, in varying degrees, in all organizations. Thus it is very important that a manager not only know, understand, and use the basic principles of good decision making, but also be completely aware of the influence of human relations on the people involved in the decision-making process (the decision maker, the data gatherers, and those from whom data are gathered).

One example of a decision based on data that do not reflect the real-world situation occurred when a leading U.S. automobile manufacturer conducted a survey to determine exactly what features the public would like incorporated in a new production automobile. The survey was made in good faith, and presumably the respondents replied in good faith. The only problem arose after the automobile was introduced to the public. Then it was clear that an error had been made, as reflected in the lack of public support in purchasing the new automobile.

What was the problem? Was the survey written so that it biased the respondents? Did the surveyors interpret the data properly? Were some results of the survey preselected? Did the manufacturer place too much faith in the company's good name? There is no irrefutable evidence to answer any of these questions. However, one strong theory is that the respondents may have given idealized answers, not answers indicating what features would actually influence the purchase decisions. For example, although an individual may cite desirable features in a new automobile, the data could be irrelevant because that person cannot afford to purchase a new automobile regardless of its features.

How do you prevent this from happening to you? Unfortunately, you cannot. But you can arm yourself with logical decision-making methods which can reduce the number of errors you will make. Since the large percentage of decisions do not involve areas in which hard data can be generated to represent the future results of various actions, you must rely on a logical decision-making process. This process should not overlook the mechanics of the methods, the people involved or affected by the decision, and, if applicable, mathematical aids for the decision maker. In previous chapters we covered these three areas. Although this book is by no means an all-inclusive, step-by-step guide for all management decisions, it certainly offers a firm foundation for the manager interested in improving her or his decision-making capabilities.

OPINION VERSUS FACT

It would be nice if all decisions could be based on facts, but is it possible? If one of your best employees states that a new employee is a dope, is that a fact? Perhaps, but as it is stated, it is not fact. It is simply the opinion of your best employee. The statement may be based on what is perceived as sound evidence, but it is still an opinion and you would be wrong to take any action based on the assumption of this "fact."

In the decision-making process, in gathering facts you should expect to obtain a number of opinions, because people with experience in a given area do not hesitate to express an opinion. To ascertain whether you are dealing with facts or opinions, find out whether you will get the same answer when you pose the same question to different sources. If you are dealing with facts, the information from both sources will be identical. If you are dealing with opinions, you can expect to get different answers. Often the question may be phrased so as to encourage a reply that is an opinion rather than a fact. For example, how many competent employees are in department X? One person might assume that everyone was competent, whereas another might spend a lot of time simply trying to decide what makes one individual competent and another incompetent.

At times, this technique can be used to good advantage, for different replies may indicate that both answers are correct when viewed from the different respondents' perspectives. As a decision maker, you must determine why these respondents disagree—not that one is right and the other wrong, but why they have different perspectives. Obviously this includes opinions different from yours. So, to analyze an opinion, start with the assumption that the opinion is correct from the respondent's perspective and to try to understand the basis from which the opinion has evolved.

If you, the decision maker, do not try to understand why differences of opinion exist, then you are guilty of approaching a decision with a closed mind. If you have a closed mind, why ask for a second opinion? Are you looking for a "yes" person whom you can blame if your decision is incorrect? Surely this is not the case. So you must be seeking opinions to substantiate what you already believe to be true. If you discard the second opinion because it fails to substantiate your belief, you are wasting your time. Usually the decision maker does not even realize that he or she is guilty of choosing a biased approach to solve a problem. Therefore, unless one (and only one) course of action is clear in the given circumstances, you should expect and even encourage disagreement. When all the people involved in making a decision agree, ask yourself, Why involve so many people if the direction could be identified just as well by a much smaller group at a much lower cost? However, if different opinions are based on conflicting perspectives and the interpretation of these views, you should be familiar with both perspectives before you decide which way to go.

One of the decision maker's primary tasks may be to encourage people to express opinions, even when these do not conform to the norm. There should be absolutely no hint that a diverse opinion will be ridiculed or any person belittled, for this may stifle the surfacing of opinions that could offer a new perspective in the decision-making process. This is extremely important when you are dealing with less agressive individuals, new employees, or people who perceive themselves to be lower in the organization's hierarchy. These individuals should know that their opinions will be evaluated on the basis of their perspective. This does not mean that you will use these opinions as a basis for a final decision, for the perspectives of these opinions may be inappropriate (too narrow, too broad, and so on).

Wild opinions having no basis other than emotion should be discouraged. For example, an engineer whose expertise lies in stress analysis certainly should voice an opinion about the structural integrity of a proposed product, but not about the market potential of the new product. The best decisions are made by seriously considering all the opinions with valid bases and then evaluating these bases.

Good decision makers know when to stop gathering opinions and facts, because the data being received tend to repeat themselves. Then they must take action. This is done with the understanding that a consensus has not been reached and so the decision may not please everyone. Thus anyone who lacks the courage to disagree with some well-intended advice should not be in a decision-making position. The decision makers' task is to do the right thing, not what they would like to do, what would make them popular, and not what they may be expected to do.

QUALITY OF THE DECISION

One reason that it is difficult to offer a clear set of "cookbook" procedures to follow for each decision relates to the evaluation of the decision's effectiveness once it has been made. Was it a good decision? Since usually you select only one course of action from a wide array, you cannot know what outcome would have resulted if a different alternative had been selected. You cannot judge the quality of a decision by its outcome, because outside influences may have affected the outcome after the decision has been reached.

In general, the quality of a decision can be represented by a bell-shaped curve. Within one standard deviation (68 percent) most decisions are acceptable, 14 percent of all decisions are poor, and 14 percent are superior. Only 2 percent are either unacceptable or outstanding. This is illustrated by Figure 63.

Figure 63 dramatically points out the large range of acceptable solutions open to the decision maker. However, the figure also illustrates the small range of superior decisions and even smaller range of outstanding ones. To make a conscious effort to improve your decision-making capability, you should concentrate on having your decisions fall as far to the right of the mean as possible. However, how far to the right should you try to move? At this point your decision-making judgment comes into play. As noted earlier, it is possible to gather more and more data about almost any question. You must judge when to stop gathering data.

One good method of deciding when you have enough data is related to the data's repeatability. The amount of repeatability depends on the

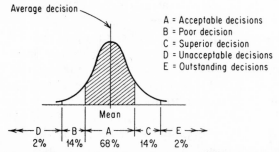

Average decision

A = Acceptable decisions
B = Poor decision
C = Superior decision
D = Unacceptable decisions
E = Outstanding decisions

Mean

D — 2%   B 14%   A 68%   C 14%   E 2%

Figure 63   Standard distribution of decision quality.

complexity and impact of the decision. For example, if you are not quite sure of the proper format for a letter, perhaps only a quick reference to a correspondence manual or a question posed to someone with more experience is required. However, if you are exploring the market potential for a product in a foreign land, then you may consult a number of experts. Once your feedback data start to repeat themselves, you know you have made one inquiry too many.

One word of caution: The repeated data should account for all viewpoints about the problem. For example, the foreign marketing firm could predict the need for your product, but be unaware that a competitor was ready to introduce a similar product or that your company could not afford the slow cash flow associated with the particular venture.

Obviously, no one wants to solicit more viewpoints than are required, because more resources are applied to solve the problem than it merits. So, how do you avoid soliciting more opinions than are needed and, at the same time, cover all critical aspects of the problem? No textbook or individual can answer this question precisely. The answer is unique to each decision and must be based on only the decision maker's judgment. This judgment, in turn, is based on many other factors, such as experience, intelligence, personality, education, timing, and so on.

One way to measure the quality of your decisions is to compare the results of your decision with your expectations prior to making the decision. To do this, you must have a clear-cut goal in mind before making a decision. This should be no problem, because you should not be involved in the decision-making process if you do not have a clear-cut set of expectations about the outcome.

THE BLACK BOX

Figure 64 shows a black box. It represents a basic decision process in which decisions are related to the method of achieving a desired goal. Figure 64 shows that a decision involves only three factors: input, output, and the process itself. The most important aspect of any decision is the desired output. This may be defined by quantity, quality, price, time, product, or any other variable.

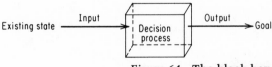

Figure 64   The black box.

Once you have defined the goal, you run through the decision process to discover how to get from your current state to the desired goal. Hence the decision process can be thought of as a plan to define the best way to reach the desired end position. This plan may include actions that must be taken and support equipment or personnel that must be instructed so that their actions cause you to move in the right direction.

Next you must find out what resources are required to implement these actions. The input requirements should be defined accordingly by the five M's: money, manpower, machinery, materials, and methods. Then you must assess the impact of applying these inputs to existing operations. You would be very shortsighted if you applied any of the five M's to achieve a goal and inadvertently disrupted another of the organization's ongoing efforts.

It is possible that you cannot devote the resources necessary to implement your plan. Should you revise the plan or the goal? First you should try to revise the plan, assuming that the goal is worthy and the necessary resources are not beyond reach. If you can modify the plan so that a different combination of the five M's is needed, you may be able to achieve your goal without an unacceptable disruption of any ongoing effort. If such modification is not possible, you should decide whether your goal needs to be modified. If it does, repeat the process just described.

Your last step (assuming that eventually you achieve a satisfactory input, process, and output) is to concentrate on the input and output. At this point ask yourself, is attaining the goal worth the necessary investment? At times you may be surprised to discover that after the goal, process, and input have been modified a number of times, the answer is "No!"

In summary, the black box process starts with a well-defined goal and works backward to determine the required inputs. By moving back and forth through the process, then, you can choose those actions that are right for the particular application. Always keep in mind that one possible action is to do nothing. This can be the most desirable choice for several reasons. The most common reason is that reaching the desired goal simply may not be worth the investment in resources.

DECISION LEVELS

Decision levels are the organizational level at which the decision maker is located and the organizational level at which decisions are made. They should coincide, but unfortunately they do not always.

Obviously an individual in the organization whose duties and responsibilities are at the journeyman level would not be involved in policy-making decisions. But sometimes it is less clear that individuals at the top of the organizational hierachy should not be involved in the nuts-and-bolts decisions. This problem is especially prominent when an individual is promoted because he or she was so effective in the previous job.

We have all heard of various sized businesses that have been built up by an individual only to fail when that person leaves the business. When this occurs in a family business, usually we assume that the parents were simply better business people than the children. But this is not always true; often the parent simply could not (or would not) delegate decision-making authority to the child. Thus the child simply does not acquire the first-hand experience of decision-making successes and failures on a small scale. By the time such a young person inherits the decision-making responsibility, many of the decisions are critical. One poor decision may be enough to sink a business under certain circumstances.

The small organization or business usually has a small number of organizational levels associated with its operations. In many cases, the organization consists of the owner-operator and the workers. The owner-operator usually understands all aspects of the business, and there is no problem of mismatched organizational and decision-making levels. In a large organization, many layers exist. Since each layer of the organization carries an increasing scope of responsibility, often it is quite difficult for the rising manager to realize that he or she no longer has the up-to-date information needed to make decisions at the lower levels. This is illustrated by Figure 65.

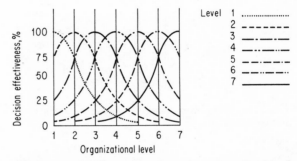

Figure 65 Decision effectiveness versus organizational level.

This figure shows that each individual is most effective at making decisions at his or her own level of responsibility. As an individual approaches the next level (up or down the organizational ladder), the effectiveness of his decisions drops off rapidly. At two levels away a person makes decisions that are only about 25 percent effective, and at farther levels they are even less effective. However, the effectiveness never reaches 0 percent.

It is interesting that in Figure 65 the effectiveness drops off in both directions. This may come as a shock to level 7 managers who believe that their decisions are effective from top to bottom in the organization because they came up through the ranks. This figure also illustrates that level 1 employees are most effective at their present positions, yet they have inputs at all levels of the organization with varying degrees of effectiveness. The effectiveness drops off not because the individual lacks the basic intelligence to analyze the facts related to the choice to be made, but rather because the individual lacks current data about all the related interactions that would be affected by the decisions.

It is obvious that this family of curves relates to a typical organization. The span of each curve may be skewed in either direction or flattened or narrowed, depending on the type of organization, the work performed, and the capabilities of the individual. Figure 66 illustrates

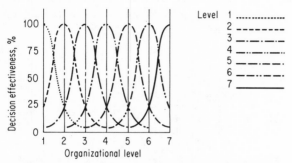

Figure 66 Technical decision effectiveness versus organizational level.

a narrower span of effectiveness than Figure 65. This should be expected in a highly technical (or specialized) work environment. In engineering, this span of effectiveness could be thought of as the technical obsolescence resulting from the completion of formal training and its application to the work environment. Although it is possible to stave off technical obsolescence by continuing part-time training, the person receiving part-time training cannot keep pace with the individual who uses this training daily.

Regardless of the span of effective decision making, it is seldom as perfectly bell-shaped as in Figures 65 and 66. The reason is thus. As individuals are promoted up the organizational ladder, at first they are more familiar with their previous jobs than with their new ones. Therefore, probably they are more effective in their old jobs. As time passes, their effectiveness increases in the new positions while decreasing in the old jobs, simply because these individuals are no longer active in their duties and responsibilities. If they aspire to the next level on the organizational ladder, then they provide more and more assistance to their supervisors, and the curve may become skewed to the right. It is extremely unlikely that individuals can be highly effective in many levels simultaneously, since normally they are involved most actively in decision making related to their own levels of responsibility.

QUALITY CIRCLES

In recent years the concept of organizational level as related to effective decision making has been recognized. It is seldom identified by these terms, but it results from U.S. companies attempting to determine why Japanese companies appear to be more productive. In addition to many cultural differences and the fact that a Japanese employee usually stays with one company for life, considerable attention has been devoted to a work group called the *quality circle*. Basically this is a group of working-level employees who voluntarily meet to discuss problems related to their work. They discuss and study methods to improve safety, habitability, productivity, cost reduction, and so on. Once the group has completed its study, it recommends to management how to solve the particular problem. It is usually in the best interests of the company to adopt these suggestions, for they result in a more effective organization. If the company does not adopt the suggestions, then management must offer the quality circle a reasonable explanation. Many times, the recommendations made by the quality circle involve changing processes that have become the normal operating procedure for a number of employees. If such changes were mandated by management, they would likely meet with considerable opposition. However, when the employees themselves recommend these changes, then they fully support the recommendations. Of course, the benefit resulting from the improved operation is shared by all the company's employees.

Some U.S. companies have difficulties when attempting to form quality circles. The cultural differences are bound to cause some problems. But perhaps one of the more significant problems is the attitude of a typical U.S. manager. After a comprehensive briefing on this concept, I once heard the top man in an organization say, "This sounds great. I'm going to put out an instruction which initiates the quality circle concept in our organization!" The point that this man missed was that quality circles are voluntary, not a management tool. However, even more significant is the fact that this man did not recognize that working-level employees are more expert and make superior decisions at their levels than he does. This respect for one another's level of responsibility and the decisions entailed is the key to effective communication and esteem across and up and down the organizational ladder.

SUMMARY

Probably no book has been written which completely covers a topic. This book is no exception. However, the intent was not to be all-inclusive, but rather to summarize the basic considerations of management-level decision making. Once the basics are understood, then it is possible to expand expertise in the area most applicable to the specific needs. Therefore, this book is only a start in the unending study of management decision making.

A manager must be familiar with the basic decision loop and its ingredients. Once these basic ingredients are recognized, attention should be paid to the character of the decision maker, both individually and in a group. Since most decisions affect people, the manager cannot ignore the human relations influence of a decision, especially when selecting a decision-making technique. The diagrammatic representation of a given problem can take a number of forms and can be an invaluable assistance in collecting and displaying the particular problem or decision parameters. A basic understanding of probability and statistics will help in graphically displaying this information.

However, after all this information is digested and the basic building blocks of decision making are understood, still one basic ingredient is necessary to make a manager into a good decision maker. This ingredient relates to the fact that there is an element of risk in all decision situations. A person who is unwilling to take risks will never succeed as a manager. A manager who is unwilling to accept the risks of occasionally making an improper decision should not be making decisions at all. A manager must have the good judgment to know how much data to gather, the intelligence to digest the data, and, most of all, the courage to make the needed decision when it entails a risk. This inner quality of courage to accept the responsibility of a decision (be it good or bad) separates commonplace from superior decision makers.

Index